Surveying and Mapping: A Manual of Simplified Techniques

Robert F. G. Spier

STUDIES IN
ANTHROPOLOGICAL METHOD

General Editors
GEORGE AND LOUISE SPINDLER
Stanford University

SURVEYING AND MAPPING:
A MANUAL OF
SIMPLIFIED TECHNIQUES

SURVEYING AND MAPPING: A MANUAL OF SIMPLIFIED TECHNIQUES

ROBERT F. G. SPIER
University of Missouri

HOLT, RINEHART AND WINSTON, INC.
New York   Chicago   San Francisco   Atlanta
Dallas   Montreal   Toronto   London   Sydney

Copyright © 1970 by Holt, Rinehart and Winston, Inc.
All rights reserved
Library of Congress Catalog Card Number: 75–118092
SBN: 03–080987–8
Printed in the United States of America
0 1 2 3 4   3   9 8 7 6 5 4 3 2 1

FOREWORD

ABOUT THE SERIES

Anthropology has been, since the turn of the century, a significant influence shaping Western thought. It has brought into proper perspective the position of our culture as one of many and has challenged universalistic and absolutistic assumptions and beliefs about the proper condition of man. Anthropology has been able to make this contribution mainly through its descriptive analyses of non-Western ways of life. Only in the last decades of its comparatively short existence as a science have anthropologists developed systematic theories about human behavior in its transcultural dimensions, and only very recently have anthropological techniques of data collection and analysis become explicit and in some instances replicable.

Teachers of anthropology have been handicapped by the lack of clear, authoritative statements of how anthropologists collect and analyze relevant data. The results of fieldwork are available in the ethnographies and they can be used to demonstrate cultural diversity and integration, social control, religious behavior, marriage customs, and the like, but clear, systematic statements about how the facts are gathered and interpreted are rare in the literature readily available to students. Without this information the alert reader of anthropological literature is left uninformed about the process of our science, knowing only the results. This is an unsatisfying state of affairs for both the student and the instructor.

This series is designed to help solve this problem. Each study in the series focuses upon manageable dimensions of modern anthropological methodology. Each one demonstrates significant aspects of the processes of gathering, ordering, and interpreting data. Some are highly selected dimensions of methodology. Others are concerned with the whole range of experience involved in studying a total society. These studies are written by professional anthropologists who have done fieldwork and have made significant contributions to the science of man and his works. In them the authors explain how they go about this work and to what end. We think they will be helpful to students who want to know what processes of inquiry and ordering stand behind the formal, published results of anthropology.

ABOUT THE AUTHOR

Robert F. G. Spier has taught at the University of Missouri since 1949. He was trained at the University of California, Berkeley (B.A. 1947) and at Harvard University (M.A. 1949; Ph.D. 1954). His research includes fieldwork with the Yokuts Indians of California, the California Chinese, midwestern Scandinavian–Americans and Dutch–Americans, and studies in Scandinavian and Dutch museums. He has directed a project sponsored by the National Science Foundation for the development of anthropometric teaching devices. He has also experimented with ultrasonic cleaning of archeologically derived materials. Although primarily a cultural anthropologist, he has a strong interest in technology—primitive, preindustrial, and modern United States. The development of technical aids for the conduct of research and teaching is of special concern to him. He is a Fellow of the American Anthropological Association, a charter member of the Society for the History of Technology, and an Advisory Editor of the journal of this society, *Technology and Culture*.

ABOUT THE BOOK

Many ethnographers and most archeologists have at one time or another in their fieldwork been required to locate buildings, ceremonial sites, excavations, and other relevant man-made or natural features both in relationship to each other and to other fixed reference points, and in both the horizontal and vertical plane. Sometimes the result is a full-fledged map, other times it is for the sake of a less detailed description of significant spatial relationships. In any event, the field ethnographer or archeologist who is faced with these problems needs to know of systematic but relatively nontechnical procedures requiring a minimum of equipment that will facilitate the production of accurate maps and the description of relevant spatial relationships. Frequently, these procedures are not learned in graduate training and the urban origins of most academics make it unlikely that even very general knowledge of the necessary techniques will be represented in the intellectual equipment of the fieldworker. The result is that most ethnographies and even some archeological reports leave much to be desired in respect to accuracy of mapping or description of spatial relationships.

This book is designed to make the techniques of surveying and mapping, using the minimum of technical equipment, available to anyone who will take a little time to study and practice. It is couched in direct, nontechnical language in an interesting and practical manner. We hope it will be practical for students and for professionals as a manual for procedures to be used in the field.

GEORGE AND LOUISE SPINDLER
General Editors
Stanford in Germany, May 1970

PREFACE

This book is offered to a heterogeneous readership in the hope of demonstrating the basic simplicity of a technical process. Armed with it, the veriest amateur can produce some semblance of a map. It will be shown that one's wits are the best equipment for such an undertaking.

The inspiration for this approach to surveying comes from my father, Leslie Spier, who was a civil engineer by initial professional training. It was he who showed me that instrumentation was an aid, not a necessity, to the process. Together we mapped several areas with a handful of stakes, a plumb line, and a couple of measuring tapes. The process took a bit longer than it would have with conventional equipment, but it served the needs of the occasion.

It is possible to substitute skill for equipment, up to a point. The methods detailed here will, of necessity, involve the use of some equipment, but the intent is to keep the equipment (and the capital investment) to a minimum.

Parts of the material in this manual were previously published in the *Newsletter* of the Missouri Archaeological Society, principally between 1954 and 1956. The serial form of publication was intended to assist amateur archeologists and to serve as an incentive to continued membership. For his assistance at that time the author owes a substantial debt to Richard O. Keslin, then editor of the *Newsletter*. For subsequent counsel, a secondary indebtedness is acknowledged to Dale R. Henning, who succeeded Dr. Keslin as editor. Both men brought to the subject the perspective of field archeologists and the inventiveness of born gadgeteers. I thank them both.

Though the original material was designed for the edification of amateur archeologists, it came to be used by neophyte professionals in summer fieldschools and other training "digs." In time, the initial stock was exhausted and pressures have arisen for reprinting and revision. To Dr. Melvin A. Fowler goes the major credit for seeing that this has come about. I appreciate his interest and his confidence.

As always, we must hold all these contributors blameless because they had no control over the final product. The errors are, consequently, solely the fault of the author.

ROBERT F. G. SPIER

Columbia, Missouri
May 1970

CONTENTS

Introduction

F ROM TIME TO TIME the need arises for the determination of the relationship between two points. It may be necessary to know how far one point
is from the other. It may be necessary to know in what direction one point
lies from the other. It may be necessary to know how far one point lies above or
below the other. It may be necessary to portray these relationships graphically.
Before any of these needs can be met it is necessary to apply the methods of surveying to the situation.

The methods of surveying and the resultant mapping of a land area are
employed by persons in many walks of life: the archeologist, the ethnographer, the
demographer, the sociologist, the Peace Corpsman, the farmer, the planner, and,
of course, the surveyor. Of these only the last, suitably licensed, may produce an
"official" land survey which is immediately recognized as being valid on deeds and
other legal documents. The work of the others is accorded greater or lesser recog-
nition according to circumstances. Such results may have no bearing on legal matters, but may be a part of studies or action for quite different purposes. About
half of those named have direct actions in mind, while the remainder will provide
basic information which may be put into action by others.

Because the applications of surveys differ widely, so may the methods and
materials employed. Not all surveys demand pinpoint accuracy. It may be quite
enough to know that the distance between two points is 87 yards rather than
261.77 feet. The order of information furnished need not exceed the order of
information sought. Under these circumstances, it will be found that the surveying
and mapping methods detailed in this volume can produce adequate results for
many purposes.

The work of the true surveyor seems esoteric and precision-oriented. His
optical instruments are the product of centuries of refinement. His standards are
the highest. He may even employ temperature control techniques to compensate
for the minute changes in tapes brought about by the changes in air temperatures.
Lately the addition of electronic surveying equipment and of satellites to survey

the earth as a whole have taken instrumentation beyond the range of ordinary knowledge. However, it must be remembered that some of the advanced instruments of which we stand in awe are directed toward undertakings far beyond our ordinary needs. To think of using some of these in order to survey a common farm field would be comparable to summoning a battleship to shoot a seagull.

For most situations, some very simple techniques have sufficed for generations, even for millennia in a few instances. The kinds of surveying with which we are concerned here have their origins in the Nile Valley at the time of the Pharoahs. The tradition was carried on into the Middle Ages and later by mine surveyors and by those responsible for canals, bridges, and large buildings. Many undertakings were carried through, using simple techniques, before the advent of equipment with true optical sighting aids. All of which is a way of saying that, for many purposes, one does not have to indulge in fancy equipment in order to get results.

Elaborate equipment, in addition to improving accuracy, is primarily convenient. Some instruments can measure, simultaneously, the direction, distance, and vertical angle to a point. This certainly speeds up the work, but each of these may be separately measured by other instruments and other techniques. It is toward these "other instruments and other techniques" that we direct our attention.

No special note is taken of differences between the English and metric systems of measurements. The text employs English measurements throughout simply because they are most familiar and convenient for the author. The change to metric is much easier than it would seem because surveyors using English measure customarily figure in feet and decimal fractions of feet (as 10.65 ft, not 10 ft and 8 in.). Shift of practice from feet and decimal feet to meters and decimal fractions of meters is very easy. It requires little more than a change in the measuring tape being used.

Throughout the book, but especially in the section on instruments, there will be references to various brands, manufacturers, and sources of goods. These are mentioned solely for the information of the reader in the same way that methods of surveying are discussed. These references are not intended either as endorsements or as condemnations. The would-be surveyor may investigate further on his own and draw his own conclusions. (See Appendix, Equipment Sources.)

Throughout the discussion of "how to," a determined effort will be made to explain "why." It is felt that the surveyor/mapper who is simply following, point by point, a set of instructions lacks a substantial understanding of what he is doing. The very essence of surveying without instruments is that one substitutes one's wits for those instruments. If one is dull then no satisfactory substitution is made. If one encounters the unusual, then one is stymied due to an inability to extemporize. In this game, knowledge is flexibility.

1

A Place in Space

THE DEMAND FOR A MAP is often felt in anthropology, most commonly by the archeologist, less commonly by the ethnographer or social anthropologist. The ability to make an adequate survey and to produce an informative map is not confined to the professional surveyor or to the cartographer; it can be done at a certain level of competence by any patient, intelligent person.

The map of the archeologist often reflects the nature of his technique on the site. If he digs by arbitrary squares and levels, then the data for a map are automatically recorded in his notes. There remains little else other than to portray these data graphically. If the archeologist digs according to certain inherent features of the sites, following house walls, streets, or fortifications, then he has a different problem. He will have to make a particular and deliberate effort at surveying and mapping.

At this point it might be well to forestall a possible terminological confusion. Surveying is sometimes used by archeologists to refer to archeological reconnaissance, reflected in a title such as "An Archeological Survey of the Lower Pecos River," or an organization known as the "California Archaeological Survey." While surveying in the sense in which we will employ it here may be a part of the activities covered by these titles, it is not necessarily central to them. One might say that archeological surveying, in some usages, bears the same relationship to excavation that prospecting bears to mining. "Surveying" in this book will be used to speak of techniques for determining the spatial relationship of places or points.

The term "mapping" is subject to less difficulty as it has not, apparently, developed any special meaning in the anthropological context. It will be used here to refer to the graphic representation of a portion of space. Such representations usually involve using symbols and other abstractions rather than being artistically representational and realistic.

The ethnographer and the social anthropologist will use surveying techniques to produce maps of such phenomena as the plans of villages, the layout of

3

gardens, the spatial organization of marketplaces, the relation between houses and shrines. It has been the rare monograph in the past which favored its readers with more than a map of the country or continent showing the general location of the people under examination, and a nominally detailed map showing their settlements, the limits of their lands, trails or other routes of communication, and the headquarters of the district officer. Much would be gained by better maps, not only for the reader of the report but for the researcher as well. The act of surveying may elicit cooperation or arouse interest, or it may run into obstacles which reveal beliefs and attitudes hitherto unsuspected. The data gathered for the map, or the resulting map, may show patterns of organization which are not evident to less thorough inspection. This other perspective, in plan or in elevation, may be as revealing as is an aerial photograph.

Lastly, the act of surveying gives the observer a reason for going over the terrain in some detail. He will have an opportunity to observe many things and to meet many people. He is not, nominally, observing these at all, but instead is studying the land. Conceivably, where local attitudes preclude any other type of investigation, surveying may be the "cover" under which the anthropologist can reach some of the goals which he has set for himself.

It is difficult to suggest what side benefits may accrue for others engaged in surveying and mapping, because these techniques are usable for such a wide variety of purposes. For some interests the pattern may flow from the data, for instance for the planner who is already faced with the grid of town layout or land allotment. The value of surveying to reveal a pattern may recommend this approach to the Peace Corpsman or anyone who is organizing an action program. We also have to consider the person who may wish to survey land, perhaps his own, to satisfy his curiosity, increase his pride of ownership, or simply as a pastime.

The resulting map of the archeological site, of the native village, of the farm, or of the estate must not be left "floating in space." Neglecting to relate the area mapped to a larger context is a common flaw in surveying, especially in those cases where the data flow rather easily from the undertaking. Thus, we have site maps which show little more than cultural materials, those things created by man. Or a map of a village will locate it only with respect to the trails leading to nearby market towns. Maps, or surveys, with this shortcoming must be "tied in" to permanent features of the landscape, preferably ones which appear on widely used maps of the area (for example, government maps). In the United States this usually means that the landmarks included in one's private survey should also appear on U.S. Geological Survey topographic maps. In Great Britain, an appropriate reference might be the Ordnance Survey sheets. In other countries, there are commonly recognized reference maps to which a survey may be related. If none of these published standards exist, then by all means include some relationship to a major, permanent landmark. This might be a large rock outcrop, a mountain peak, a stream fork (not in flat country where stream beds may readily shift), or a canyon. If the survey area lies within a municipality, the best landmarks would be the bench marks which are a part of the governmental surveying system. Lacking access to these, it is probably wiser to use the street grid (the intersections of centerlines of street, not their margins) than to use isolated features such as monuments or buildings. One has to make an educated guess about their permanence or the manner in which they would be altered if change occurs.

The techniques which are used to survey features within the area of the map may generally be applied to relate the map as a whole to the rest of the world. It is usually not feasible or necessary to use some radically different approach to tie in the survey. Whatever the technique, the results should make it possible for a stranger to locate any feature on your map working from information conveyed by the map alone. If he needs assistance from any other source, then you have fallen short of perfection in your endeavor. You have not properly described your place in space.

2

Sticks and String

ONE OF THE MOST COMMON EXCUSES for failure to make an adequate survey, or even any survey at all, is the lack of instruments. For example, an African farm manager, seeking overseas advice on draining his lands, wrote "I guess that the way that we can remedy that situation is for me to draw a diagram of how the field lies and so forth but the problem here is that we don't have a transit and don't have any ideas as to how to make one . . . and consider the problem closed unless you have some ideas for a transit." He was advised to make a chain survey which required no instruments.

Admittedly, the standard surveying instruments, such as transit or alidade (costing $800 to $1200), are not within the reach of most individuals. Loans may be difficult to arrange and purchase may be out of the question. These are expensive items to have for occasional use and their inclusion in a research budget is unjustified unless surveying and mapping are the focus of the endeavor. Additionally, if instruments are obtained, they have to be transported to the site and could take a substantial part of one's precious baggage allowance.

In the absence of conventional instruments, there are, within the reach of everyone, items which can be used to produce maps of substantial accuracy. Some of these items are regular surveyors' equipment, others are intended for quite different uses. All of them, when applied with care, insight, and imagination, can perform some remarkable tasks. They range, as will be seen, from rather crude devices of virtually no cost to others which are more refined and more expensive, but cost is not a strict measure of utility. Accuracy is as much the product of the skill and care of the surveyor as it is a result of his choice of instruments.

Generally speaking, the techniques employed do not vary as much as do the instruments. Certain approaches are basic and they may be carried out with a variety of means. As noted above, the more expensive instruments have two merits: superior accuracy, and the ability to take several measures simultaneously. If greater accuracy is not necessary, then this attribute is superfluous. If one is patient enough to make several determinations successively instead of simultaneously, then this latter function can also be done without. We will direct our attention to those techniques which can be accomplished with simpler instrumentation. The choice of tools and techniques must be integrated.

Before considering the "sticks and string" approach to surveying we might devote some attention to conventional instruments of low cost. If these are available, then by all means use them. There is little merit in choosing the more difficult route. Although the surveying and mapping techniques we will consider are intended to be followed without these instruments, there will be no problems in adapting the methods to other gear.

The Magnetic Compass

Compasses are of debatable value for the kind of surveying which we will consider. Most of them do not read horizontal angles with sufficient definition to be useful except in wide-ranging surveys. As an example of the situation, the author's Army-type lensatic compass (made by W. and L. E. Gurley, a very reputable firm) is marked in 5° increments. The sighting line is broad enough to occupy 3° of angle. The lensatic compass, designed for cross-country marching, is rounded on the outside so that there is no side parallel to its main axis. Under these circumstances this compass cannot be used in the style of an alidade despite its sighting leaves. Its major merit is its low price (about $4) for value received. (See Fig. 1.)

The Silva-type compass is more expensive than the lensatic, being about $15, but it has the advantage of a base plate with sides parallel to the line of sight. This feature facilitates the transfer of direction to a map. (See Fig. 2.)

Close to the top in price among the compasses is the Forester's and Geologist's Compass, about $90 if you can find one. This compass has folding leaf sights and a square base aligned with the sights. It is well suited for use on the plane table except for the shortness of the sides, less than 5 in. To a degree this shortcoming can be overcome by placing a parallel-sided ruler alongside the compass base to extend the effective length of the side. One problem with this method is that the edge of the base is bevelled and is not the best bearing surface for the ruler. (See Fig. 3.)

Properly honored among the compasses is the Brunton compass, or pocket transit, which costs about $60 with a case. It has been used by generations of fieldmen. In addition to the compass needle and sighting leaves, it has a level and a clinometer for measuring the angle of slopes. It can be mounted, with the aid of a special clamp, on a tripod or on a single (Jacob) staff. (The special socket, staff, and tripod cost about $15, $10, and $25, respectively.) A major drawback is the lack of a long side parallel to the line of sight. Therefore the instrument can be used, in some ways, like a transit, but makes a poor substitute for an alidade. It is, nonetheless, considered by many to be the best of the compasses. (See Figs. 4a and 4b.)

Remember that a compass gives a magnetic bearing, not a "true" bearing. The difference between the two bearings is called the declination and should be determined, if possible, for the place of the survey. Once the information is found, on a standard survey map, aeronautical chart, or from some other source, then it may be applied to correct magnetic bearings so that the resulting map will be oriented on true bearings. If all else fails, one might try using the North Star (Polaris), if visible, as a reference for true north, but remember that it has the apparent motion of a 2° circle.

No effort will be made here to discuss the transit even though, for our purposes, it falls in the same class as the compass. As transit levels of various kinds

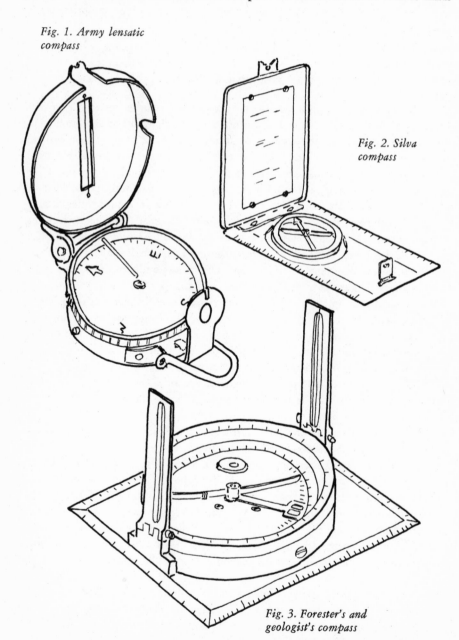

Fig. 1. Army lensatic compass

Fig. 2. Silva compass

Fig. 3. Forester's and geologist's compass

can be bought from mail-order companies, we will assume that anyone who is able to so equip himself has little need for our counsel.

All of the compasses will not only indicate direction in an absolute sense, but may also be used to measure angles included between two directions. For our purposes it is this latter ability which is of most value.

The Sighting Board

The compass, or the transit for that matter, can measure an unknown horizontal angle. It can also lay out a known angle. Both of these tasks can be performed without either compass or transit, although admittedly in a more laborious fashion. The only technical tool needed in this noninstrumental technique is a protractor. (One of adequate quality costs $1 or less.) A sighting board is made of a piece of plywood, perhaps 15 in. square. A brad or bank pin is stuck into the top as a base sighting post. A second pin is placed in the board so that it lies on the line of sight from the base sighting pin to the first target. Then a third pin

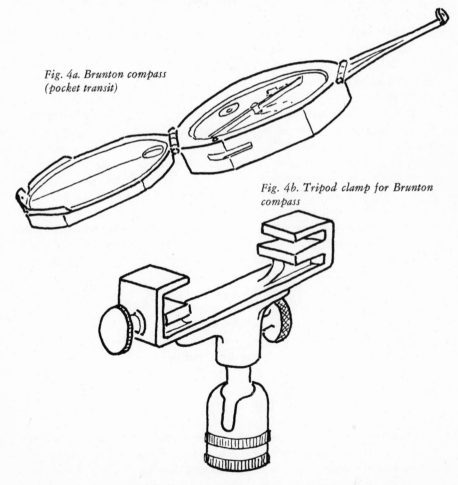

Fig. 4a. Brunton compass (pocket transit)

Fig. 4b. Tripod clamp for Brunton compass

is set so that it lies on the line from the base sighting pin to the second target. The included angle, with the base sighting pin at the vertex, is then measured with the protractor. If this is to be done with many angles, it will be found a very slow process. A paper fastened to the sighting board on which the several lines of sight may be marked as the sights are taken will enable postponement of the actual measurement until a later time when all can be done at one sitting. The paper then serves as a record of one's observations. (See Fig. 5.)

If known angles are to be laid out, they may be marked in advance on the board or its paper cover. The pins or brads are set successively on the marked angles as sighting devices. Lastly, it will greatly facilitate matters if the sighting board can be mounted on a tripod or other portable, steady support.

As an illustration of this technique in practice let us consider the following. In the author's subdivision there is a determination of the front corner of a lot (which is on the turn-around of a dead end street) by an angle measured from the centerline of the street. Often a point like this can be reached in some other way, but this was foreclosed by the absence of "irons" (surveyors' steel stakes) at crucial points. Lacking a transit, the sighting board was employed. A 235° angle was measured with the protractor, the pins set, and the board mounted on a light-weight camera tripod. The results of this exploratory survey were later confirmed by the findings of a licensed surveyor. It worked.

In using the sighting board it is best to place the angle-marking pins as far as possible from the base sighting pin. A longer sighting base is created and your accuracy improved. So place your pins as far apart as the board allows.

It is not difficult to elaborate the sighting board to make it a quick-reading device. The protractor is worked into the basic device instead of being applied after the fact. (See Fig. 6.) A full circle protractor (or two semi-circular protractors) is mounted at the base sighting pin. A second sighting pin is set at the 360° mark. These form the base line from which other angles are read. The third pin is fastened on one end of a fine wire which is fastened at the other end to the base sighting pin; the third pin is then free to swing on the radius of the wire. The sighting board is turned to align the 360° line with the base sight. The third pin is then swung into line with its target and stuck lightly into the board. The angle is read at the point where the taut wire crosses the scale of the protractor.

For those who are even more interested in building or adapting equipment, a pelorus or a sighting circle presents other possibilities. Devices like this may be found from time to time in military surplus sales.

There are limits to how far one wants to go in this direction. Our intent is to see how much we can do with how little, not to re-invent the transit!

The Alidade

At several points above, reference has been made to the alidade. Basically this instrument consists of a sighting device with a parallel straight edge on its mounting base. In use the alidade rests on a level drawing board, called a plane table, and its sights are directed toward the target. An appropriate line, guided by the side of the mounting base, is drawn on the paper covering the board. More will be said below about this technique; for the moment let us concentrate on the instrument.

The simplest type of alidade is the leaf-sight (or traverse) alidade which has a folding sight, somewhat like an adjustable rear gunsight, at each end of the base. This alidade has not been made for possibly 20 years, but occasional examples have shown up on the used market. Some have also appeared in military surplus. You are urged to seize the opportunity should one come your way. (See Fig. 7.)

Elaborations of the alidade appear in a variety of refinements: (1) the addition of an optical sighting system; (2) the equipping of these optics with stadia hairs to read distances when directed toward a standard rod; (3) the provision of a level in the base; (4) the pivoting of the telescope to read vertical angles; (5) the addition of a level for the telescope; (6) the mounting of a trough compass on the base; and (7) the addition of a prism to the eyepiece so the surveyor does not have to stoop to bring his eye to instrument level. The two basic designs of alidade, the regular and the "expedition" or "exploration," differ in the height of the telescope mount; the expedition type has a lower mount resulting in a more compact instrument. Whatever the refinement, it adds to the flexibility and convenience of use, but at a price. Distance and vertical angles can be measured in other, cheaper ways. The level stance of the plane table can be

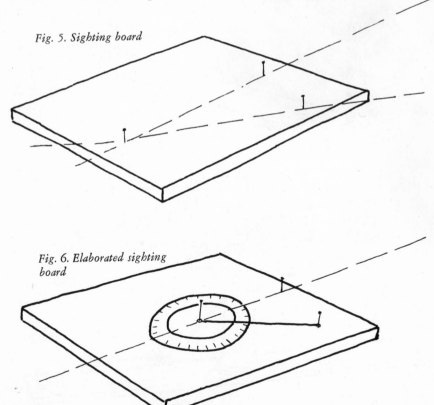

Fig. 5. Sighting board

Fig. 6. Elaborated sighting board

determined with separate levels and a separate compass will find its magnetic orientation. (See Fig. 8.)

It should be kept in mind that the purpose of an alidade is to provide the surveyor with a pair of sights through which he may look at his target, and a straight edge exactly parallel to his line of sight along which he may draw a line connecting his station (the location of his table) to the location of the target. The slight offset between his sights and the straight edge makes no difference as long as it is consistently present. This consistency is provided by drawing the lines along only one side of the straight edge, usually the right side for a right-handed surveyor.

Considering the bare essentials of the alidade, several types of improvisation spring to mind. Undoubtedly, the simplest would be a straight-edged piece of wood with two pins driven into the upper surface at exactly the same distance from the working edge. A brass-edged wooden ruler might be the base. A couple of small metal blades or small hinges could be fastened to the wooden base to form sights. One of the hinges may be slotted, preferably with a jeweler's saw (finer than a hacksaw), while the other has a fine wire soldered or cemented across an opening.

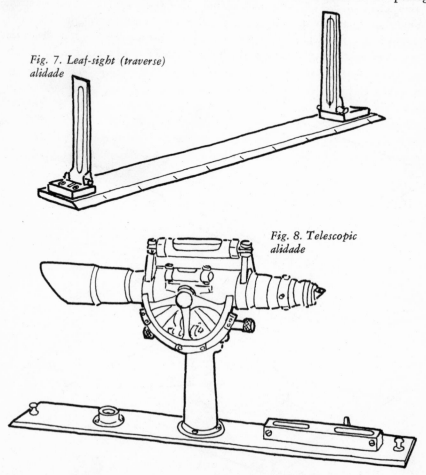

Fig. 7. Leaf-sight (traverse) alidade

Fig. 8. Telescopic alidade

This would give you a pair of sights comparable to those of field compasses or the leaf-sight alidade. (See Figs. 9a and 9b.)

A further elaboration might be made with a telescopic gun sight mounted on a metal base. Even a one-power scope would be an improvement over open sights. The cost, compared to that of a true telescopic alidade, is very small. The limits on the design and execution of homemade alidades are the imagination and the skill of their makers. (See Fig. 10.)

· A carpenter's or machinist's level, equipped with sights, would make a good expedient alidade. It would have the merit of level sighting as well as directional sighting. Additionally, it would be immediately at hand to level the plane table when beginning operations. Considering the size of the plane table and the probable weight of the level, a limit of 24 in. must be placed on the length. Many good aluminum-bodied levels, some with adjustable glasses, are now on the market. At least one tool company made sights which may be clamped to the top of a level. (Level Sights, Catalogue No. 138, Stanley Tools, New Britain, Conn.) Homemade sights would be no more difficult to attach to this base than to any other. As with any instrument, manufactured or homemade, wisdom dictates a check on its accuracy. (See Figs. 11a and 11b.)

Two methods may be used to check the accuracy of an alidade. In one method you drive two pins vertically into the surface of the plane table board, as far apart as possible, but not to exceed the length of the working edge of the instrument. The board is turned until the pins are aligned with a target 200 or more feet distant. The alidade is set against the pins. It should be aimed at the same target. Alternatively, three points along a straight line on the ground may be found or established by sighting; optimally they should be at least 200 ft apart. The plane table is set up at the middle point. Pins are set to sight over the table, in one direction at one end point, in the other direction at the other end point. The

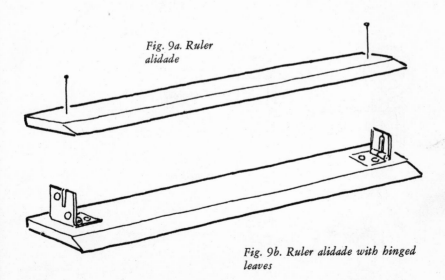

Fig. 9a. Ruler alidade

Fig. 9b. Ruler alidade with hinged leaves

alidade is then sighted successively at these points. The test, in one form or the other, should be run several times starting with the alignment of the sighting pins. A consistent error, to one side, will be due to the alidade. If any instrument adjustment can be made, then do so. If no adjustment can be made to the instrument, then no compensation will need to be made if the entire survey is conducted with this instrument to set directions. Note that an adjustment will have to be accounted for when the north line is marked on the resultant map.

Periodic checks should be run on the condition of all instruments even though the techniques of use are designed to prevent the accumulation of errors.

The Angle Prism

A suitably mounted prism for sighting angles of 90° is quite convenient for simple surveying and layout work. The prisms are compact, light, accurate, and comparatively cheap.

The prisms come in three forms: a simple right angle prism; a right angle mirror arrangement using two mounted mirrors; and a double right angle prism. Each has its particular merits. Each is usually mounted so that a plumb bob may be attached to the handle.

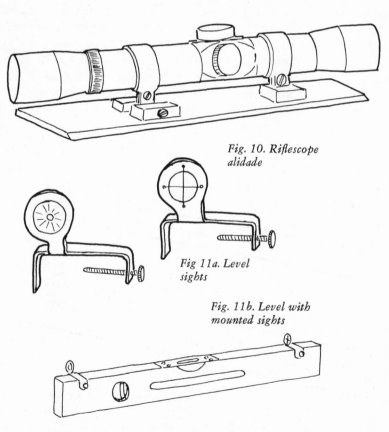

Fig. 10. Riflescope
alidade

Fig 11a. Level
sights

Fig. 11b. Level with
mounted sights

A prism is nothing which one should try to make, but unmounted prisms of suitable characteristics are available at modest prices. One source is the Edmund Scientific Company (Barrington, New Jersey) which also offers a penta prism already mounted for this service. The prices of prisms range from less than $2 up to $8. Mounted prisms from surveying equipment firms cost $20 to $50.

The right angle double mirror is an instrument which can be easily improvised in the field. It consists of two small mirrors which are set, reflective surfaces opposing, with an included angle of 45°.

When you look into one mirror to see the image of the other, an object viewed through this double reflection will be at a 90° angle to your original line of sight. Thus, you hold the mirror device at eye level and look simultaneously through the mirror system and over it. The mirror image is then aligned with a point on your main line of sight. (See Figs. 12a and 12b.)

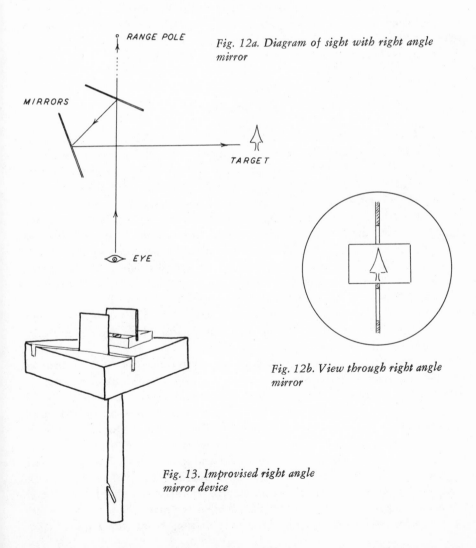

Fig. 12a. Diagram of sight with right angle mirror

RANGE POLE

MIRRORS

TARGET

EYE

Fig. 12b. View through right angle mirror

Fig. 13. Improvised right angle mirror device

The device illustrated was made from a small block of wood, a second wood scrap, a wood screw, a piece of dowel, and two bits of mirror. One mirror is set permanently into a sawcut in the block. The other mirror is mounted on a bit of wood pivoted on the screw; it can be adjusted to the proper angle by swinging around that pivot. (See Fig. 13.) You adjust your instrument by taking a sight and then a reverse sight, in the other direction, using the same sight line and the same lateral target. When these coincide without further adjustment of the movable mirror you know it is set properly. A slot is provided in the handle to hold a plumb line.

Though the prototype was precision manufactured, this replica is the ultimate in simplicity. It can be elaborated by improving the mounts, by furnishing a protective cage, and by using front silvered mirrors.

There are many times when it is quicker in surveying to figure a point to the survey by taking an offset than by direct inclusion. By offsetting you can readily include points which lie to each side of the survey line at a reasonable distance. Another use of the offset is to carry a survey line around an obstable and return to the original line. The prisms greatly facilitate both maneuvers.

The Plane Table

The plane table is used, in conjunction with the alidade or its substitute, to draw a map in the field. This technique is called plane tabling and is done concurrently with the process of surveying, not afterward. The rough field map may be perfected later, but it is substantially complete when the survey is finished.

Physically the plane table consists of a flat wooden board, like a drawing board, mounted on a substantial tripod. Traverse boards are small, 15 in. square or 18 by 24 in., and equipped with a trough compass in one edge. (The traverse board is used with the leaf-sight, or traverse, alidade which lacks its own trough compass.) Other plane table boards, for use with optically-sighted alidades, range up to 24 by 31 in. All boards have recessed screws to hold the paper with which the board is covered in use. All boards have a socket plate on the underside to couple to the tripod. Prices of this equipment run $25 to $50 for the boards and $100 or more for the tripods. Obviously this is an area where expedients are in order. (See Fig. 14.)

The trough compass referred to above, and in connection with refinements of alidades, has a magnetic needle mounted in a narrow housing (or trough). It has a very restricted swing, through about 6°, and is used solely to orient the board in a north-south direction. Its place may be readily taken by an ordinary compass unless some gadgeteer wants to make his own trough compass for installation in a board. It should have a lock to stop the needle when not in use. (See Fig. 15.)

While in use the plane table drawing board must be level. The professional alidade has a circular bubble level mounted on its blade (base or shoe) with which this leveling process is done. The amateur surveyor may wish to have a small level in his kit because his alidade, if any, will doubtless not have a built-in level. Someone who has troubled to equip his homemade drawing board with a trough compass may additionally wish to incorporate a level. There are many designs of small camera and machine levels which are suitable.

When one comes to consider homemade plane tables, one starts with the board. The standard draftsman's drawing board is so cheap, about $5, that it seems foolish to turn to anything else. However, there are two considerations which might lead you in another direction. First, the draftsman's board is usually of basswood which is very soft and readily dented. (Some dents in soft woods can be steamed out or reduced by use of a damp blotter or cloth and a regular clothes iron. Place the blotter over the dent and press with the hot iron.) The plane table board is of white pine, somewhat harder than basswood, and may have hardwood reinforcing cleats at the ends. Second, the plane table board may be awkward to haul along into the field. One might plan to use as the plane table one large side of a packing case. It will probably be of plywood, which is not the best choice, but still is serviceable. If this is planned, put the best surface of the plywood on the inside

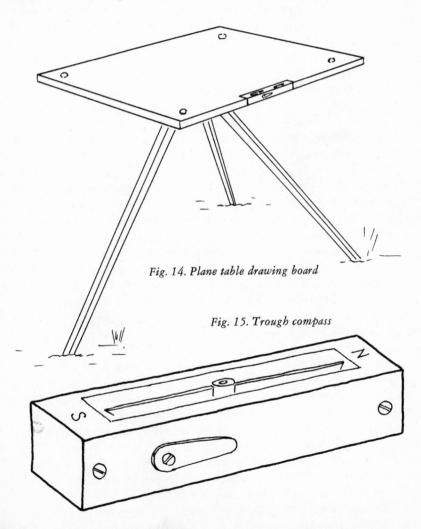

Fig. 14. Plane table drawing board

Fig. 15. Trough compass

of the packing case so it does not get gouged in transit. Neither the trough compass nor the paper-securing studs are vital, so just ignore them.

The tripod presents greater problems. A camera tripod is generally not suitable for use with the plane table. In the first place only the most massive camera tripod approximates the substantial tripods used with surveying equipment. Secondly, the camera tripod head terminates in a screw (usually one-quarter inch diameter by twenty threads to the inch, that is, 1/4–20) which is too small to withstand the torque developed by weight on the edge of the plane table board. Besides, it is most likely that any investigator worth his salt will be using his camera tripod with his camera.

This, then, is a place where ingenuity will be strained to the utmost. The basic requirements are that the board shall be held at a convenient height for the surveyor, and that the board should be capable of being tilted and pivoted so as to level and orient it properly.

A convenient height for the surveyor will, obviously, vary from one individual to the next. The plane tabler must be able to reach across the board to draw lines and make measurements without leaning on the edge. He must also be able to look through the sights of his alidade without undue stooping. Ignoring the complications introduced by use of a prismatic eyepiece, as on a telescopic alidade, a height of about 40 in. seems reasonable. This would call for a tripod with a leg length of 54 to 60 in. A fixed length leg for the tripod is far easier to contrive than is an extension or telescoping leg. If you have a good perspective drawing and several photographs of a stiff-legged tripod, probably the village carpenter can duplicate the item for you.

The tripod head and the attachment to the board present a problem. Contact between head and board might be best by way of two rings, 4 to 6 in. in diameter, which bear one on the other. This will give a more stable and stronger mount than the use of a central screw alone. A means of clamping the rings together around their peripheries can be provided, but a central screw will do the same job in satisfactory style because the strain isn't concentrated on the screw. (See Fig. 16.)

The ring-to-ring (or disk-to-disk) mount will enable rotation of the table for orientation, but will do nothing to facilitate leveling. A simple, but not easy, way to level the board would be by setting the tripod legs. It would be some improvement to have two of the tripod legs adjustable for length. If that is the approach to leveling, then one might just as well plan to use a tripod with three adjustable legs.

One type of leveling head for a tripod uses a spherical section which rests in a flat ring. The rim of the fractional sphere is drawn by a central bolt against a plate on the underside of the plane table board. The spherical section is held into the ring-rest by the bolt which also passes through another spherical section (its concave side up as well) which is drawn against the underside of the ring. The ring has on its edge the lugs to which the tripod legs are fastened. The whole assembly is actually more elaborate, in its patented form, than the description above, but this reduction will suffice. It provides a modified ball-and-socket joint with a limited degree of freedom to adjust the plane of the board. (See Fig. 17.)

Because of the difficulties with tripods, it is suggested that the hardware (which can be purchased separately) for the desired type of tripod be taken into the field. The wooden parts can be made on the spot and need not be hauled to some remote place.

As a final caution, please note that the tripod fittings, as well as those on the plane table board itself, should be of nonmagnetic metals. You may want to use a compass on the board some of the time.

Levels

A map is drawn on a flat piece of paper, but the world is not. Even if it were "flat," as some people still believe it to be, instead of spheroidal, there would remain the relief of the immediate terrain. Proper surveying requires that cognizance be taken of these ups and downs.

It should be noted that surveying proceeds, in one way, as though one were dealing with a flat world. Measurements of distances are always taken with the tape or other measuring device level with the horizon. On a steep slope the horizontal distance measured is substantially less than the distance over the surface of the ground. The surface distance is the hypotenuse of a triangle. In taking measurements with the tape, the downhill end is held level with one hand while a plumb line is held in the other hand. The plumb line is held so that the string lies vertically past the tape. When the plumb bob is on the mark, the distance is read where the line crosses the tape. The uphill end of the tape can usually be juxtaposed to the mark at ground level.

Only under the most primitive circumstances or in response to special needs would one dispense with the surveying of elevations. The elevation is the height of a given point on the land's surface above a base plane (or datum). Customarily

Fig. 16. Plane table mounting ring   Fig. 17. Plane table leveling head

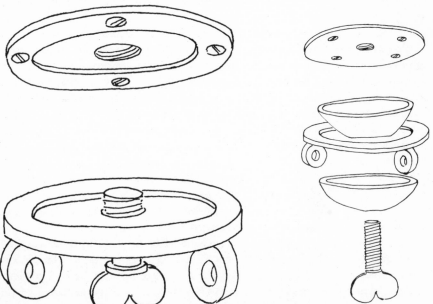

the base is mean sea level. Fortunately for those living inland it is not necessary to run a leveling traverse from a seacoast. The standard survey of most countries has determined the elevation of various key points and established at these points markers called "bench marks." The U.S. Geological Survey and the U.S. Coast and Geodetic Survey have set markers of this kind in many parts of the United States; their location is shown on topographic and other high grade maps. The mark on the map is usually a small triangle containing a dot or a small x with the letters BM and a number next to the mark. (The number is the elevation, usually in feet.) The actual bench mark is a bronze disk set into a permanent base. On it may be marked the elevation in feet. Lacking such notation you will have to refer to published maps.

Aside from the bench marks there are other sources of elevation information, some of it only approximate. The elevation of the local railroad station is usually known to railroad men, especially in the western United States, and may be marked on timetables. The elevation of the local airport is known to persons connected with it and is marked on the aeronautical charts. Because the range of television and frequency modulated (FM) radio stations is dependent upon antenna height, the management of these stations is very likely to know the elevation at the base of transmitting towers. A stable lake level might be your datum. Finally, the highway departments usually have information on the elevation of major highway features such as bridges, tunnels, and intersections.

Failing all the usual sources of elevation information, the surveyor may have to establish his own datum, or base level. In this instance the preferable landmark is something large, permanent, and shown on an official survey. (As aerial surveys are increasingly used to control mapping of remote areas, the point chosen could well be one which will be revealed in an aerial photograph.) For convenience in the field survey, additional bench marks can be established in a temporary fashion. They must be tied in, eventually, to the best available general survey of the area.

The conventional means of measuring elevation differences between points (instrument or plane table stations) is to take a level sight against a marked leveling rod. The rod is marked, usually, in feet and tenths of a foot and the level sight tells the height of the instrument above the ground on which the rod rests. The telescopic sights of a transit or alidade are equipped with a central crosshair and the reading is easy to take. With open sights it is not so easy. It may be desirable for the rodman to hold his hand or a white card against the rod as a target; the rodman will probably have to read the rod and relay the information back to the instrument man.

Leveling is one surveying process in which amateur methods and expedient devices may do as well as those of the professional. People have been making and using levels for millennia, perhaps longer than any other surveying device. The approach chosen will have some bearing on the means employed.

If one wishes to duplicate the conventional leveling methods, then a level line of sight is needed, as is a leveling rod. The level line of sight, for the amateur surveyor, may be established with the aid of a carpenter's or other long level equipped with sights. (Such an instrument was mentioned in the discussion of the alidade.) A problem is encountered in looking through the sights and observing the level's glass at the same time. The old style wooden carpenter's level, with a glass set into one long edge, is easy to use in this way because a small mirror can be mounted to reflect the image of the bubble. If the mirror has some of its silver backing scraped away, it can be on the sight line. With a modern metal-bodied level, some other mirror mount will have to be used and the surveyor will look alternately at the mirror and at the sights. (See Fig. 18.)

It is not necessary to use a manufactured level when one can be easily made from scrap materials. Variations of the following device have been used for the past 4000 years in the Near Eastern area. It can be made with three sticks, five nails, a stone, a wire, and a piece of string. Even this list can be reduced by sub- stituting lashings and pegs for the nails. The gadget is basically an isosceles triangle, ⅄ with the base upward. If a plumb bob is hung from the midpoint of the upper side, then this side will be level when the plumb line crosses the bottom point of the triangle. The triangle does not have to be precisely constructed because an approximation will suffice for the frame. Two nails are driven part way into the face of the frame, one at each upper corner. Then, using the wire (a string would be too stretchy) and a nail as a compass, scribe two arcs of equal radius using these corner nails as the centers. These arcs should intersect on the triangular frame near the bottom corner. This point is marked. By a series of trial-and-error arcs of smaller radii, find the midpoint of the upper side. Drive a nail part way into the frame here. From this midpoint you suspend the stone (or other weight) on the string. When using this leveling frame, the surveyor sights across the upper corner nails and his assistant watches the device from the side to see that the plumb line hangs across the lower mark, that the device is being held level. Possibly some gadgeteer can devise a system of mirrors so he can watch the plumb line himself while taking the horizontal sight. (See Fig. 19.)

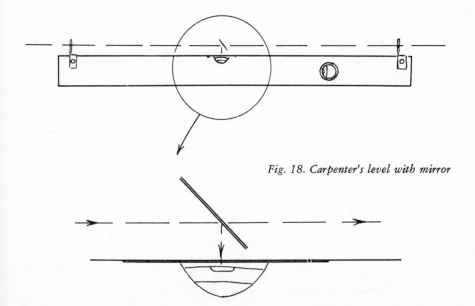

Fig. 18. Carpenter's level with mirror

The same device can be used as a simple level, not as a sighting device, when it is turned with the point up instead of down. Some adjustment will have to be made to the plumb bob so that it doesn't strike the ground. Otherwise the principle and operation remain the same. (See Fig. 20.)

For leveling at short distances, with 100 ft as a possible limit, an ordinary garden hose will do a fine job. The hose is filled with water and the ends elevated, tied to stakes, at the points to be checked for level. Because water stands level, simple measurements between the water level (not the hose end) and the ground will show the difference in level, if any, between the two points. This technique, while basically simple, can be difficult because the water has a tendency to surge

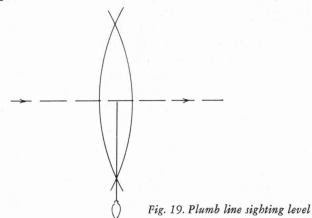

Fig. 19. Plumb line sighting level

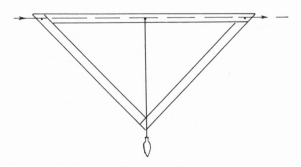

Fig. 20. Plumb line surface level

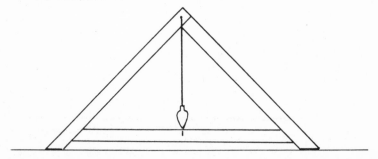

in the hose. It is much easier if a transparent or translucent hose is used so that the water level doesn't have to reach close to the open end of the hose. The Dutch, and other Europeans, sell a factory-made water level which has sight glasses (like those on a boiler) with valves at the ends of a flexible tube. The sight glasses are calibrated to facilitate measurements; they do not have to be marked for simple leveling. (See Fig. 21.)

Speaking of water leveling, you might keep in mind the uses which may be made of a bowl full of water. The surface of the water will always be level, so a line of sight across the surface, with the bowl brimful, will also be level. A straight stick resting on a wooden block floating in the bowl will also provide you with a level line of sight. If the stick and block are not evenly balanced, they will list in one direction or another. However, this tilt is readily checked and corrected by sighting at the same target alternately from opposite ends of the stick. The stick and float are revolved and adjusted until the sight line is the same from both ends. Then one knows it is truly level. A great deal can be done with a level of this kind. (See Fig. 22.)

In addition to various homemade levels, for which we have not exhausted all possibilities, there are ready-made ones of varying cost. If you wanted to run a string between the points to be leveled, then a line level could be hung at its midpoint. This method is rather inaccurate for distances of more than 25 ft. However, it could be enough for the occasion.

Hand levels are available in several patterns. One style is basically tubular with a small telescope in the tube. On the top of the tube is a bubble level which is seen from below, through the telescope, by means of a prism. Thus one may sight the crosshairs of the telescope on a target and simultaneously watch the bubble. Some hand levels are flat on the bottom so that they may be used as contact levels as well; this type has advantages when used with a plane table. (See Fig. 23a.)

The Abney level is an elaborate hand level with the bubble mounted on a movable arc. This level may be used to sight along slopes in addition to level sighting. On a slope the target is sighted through the telescope and the arc is shifted until the bubble reads level. The slope, in degrees or some other appropriate unit, is read from the arc. (See Fig. 23b.)

Both the surveyor's common hand level and the Abney level may have their telescopes equipped with stadia hairs. These aid in measuring distances and will be discussed in the appropriate section.

The Brunton pocket transit, when used to measure the angle of slopes (that is, as a clinometer), makes use of a bubble level. The sights are trained on the target and then the clinometer section is revolved until the bubble reads level. The slope, in degrees or percent of grade, is read from the scale. In effect the Abney level and the Brunton operate on the same principle. Both may be used to take level sights.

The pendulum clinometer is used primarily for sighting on slopes, but may be used for level sighting. The shell of this instrument is a shallow cylinder with a peep hole in its curved wall and a sight window directly opposite. Within the drum is mounted a pendulum which carries a translucent scale marked in degrees. The arc of the pendulum is limited, 45° in each direction, by stops and checked by a brake which must be released by finger pressure when using the instrument. Inside, the surveyor sees the scale and the index mark by way of a magnifying mirror. As he looks through, he sees the scale, the index mark, and the target. Aligning the index mark with the target, he reads the adjacent scale. The handle of the clinometer is at the bottom, in a flat boss on which the instrument may rest when being used as a contact level. (See Fig. 24.)

An angle prism or angle mirror device, mentioned above with the direction-sighting items, can be used as an expedient level. The cord of a plumb bob is looped around the upper handle of the prism and the prism itself held horizontally at eye level. When the bob stops oscillating, the image of the cord will mark a level line on the line of sight. The image can then be aligned, looking past the prism (mirrors), with the target. What is done is to take a sight at right angles to the plumb line, which is vertical, giving a horizontal line of sight.

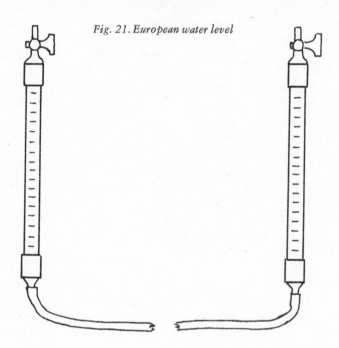

Fig. 21. European water level

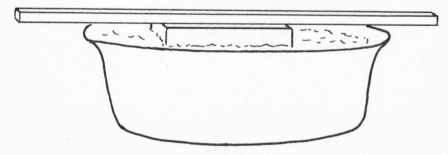

Fig. 22. Floating sighting stick

None of the hand-held levels is very convenient for lengthy use. It may be to the surveyor's advantage to have a staff on which to rest the level. If this is made 5 ft long, or another whole number, it can be kept in one's calculations rather easily as a constant.

Surveyor's levels of several kinds show up occasionally in military surplus sales. Unless you disdain them as factory products when you are managing on a home-made basis, they are well worth considering. Also, a word of caution about the variety of patent levels now on the market. Despite the claims of their sellers, some of them are not worth much. If you are going to buy a level, it would be well to compare the cost of a professional hand level of proven quality with that of some plastic gadget.

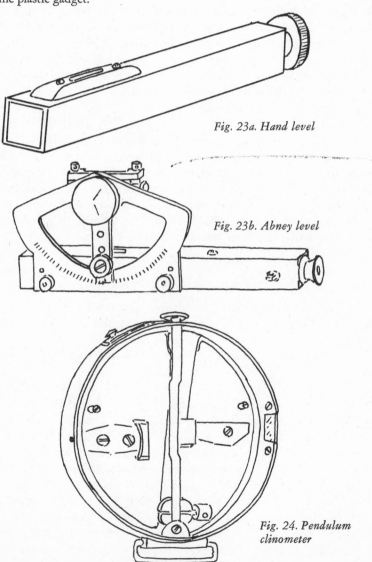

Fig. 23a. Hand level

Fig. 23b. Abney level

Fig. 24. Pendulum clinometer

Leveling Rods

Normally in leveling work, the level is used in conjunction with a rod bearing graduations reading from the ground upward. The graduations are usually in feet and hundredths of a foot; in metric measure, the marks are in meters and centimeters. The more elaborate rods have verniers which make it possible to read to 0.001 ft. None of these marks can be seen with open sights or low-powered optical systems. Consequently you would be advised to use marking at foot and half-foot intervals or, if finer measure is desired, at foot and tenth intervals.

The rod itself could be 6 to 12 ft long. Standard rods are of about this size. To make them more portable, the sections of a rod may collapse by sliding past each other. Or the rod may be folding, with one hinge, or the rod may be in jointed sections. Probably your easiest joint would be a folding one with a hinge. When the rod is straightened out, it can be held rigid by a batten across the hinged joint. One merit of the jointed rod, not to be overlooked for the sake of other advantages, is that one or two sections can be used when a shorter rod will suffice. It will reduce the work of the rodman.

A leveling rod can be a most unhandy piece of baggage. For those who wish to travel light, and possibly for others, there is made a so-called flexible leveling rod. This consists solely of a high grade rod facing which may be tacked on any suitable backing. It is precisely marked, in English or metric measure, and costs about $10. In transit the facing is rolled compactly. The flexible rod is offered in several lengths and two widths by most major surveyor's supply firms. For the person who wants precision leveling without the labor of measuring and painting his own rod face, these rods offer a great bargain.

Tapes and Other Distance Measures

The measurement of distance in surveying proceeds either by direct measurement or by some indirect ranging method. Direct measurements are simplest, most common, and most obvious. We will begin with them.

Pacing of distances requires no equipment whatsoever. Any individual's natural walking stride is quite constant over hard, level surfaces and can yield surprisingly accurate results. There will be some variation over rough ground, on a slope or when carrying a load. The most difficult part of pacing is to continue to walk naturally while keeping a count of paces. There is a tendency for the pacer to immediately assume a self-conscious stride when pacing. Do not try to develop a special mode of striding to pace distances. It requires constant attention to maintain this stride and you will probably have your mind occupied with other things.

The counting of paces may be simplified if you count only every other pace, on the right foot if you stepped off with the left. It is possible, through practice, to develop the faculty of counting almost unconsciously. One may use a handful of small stones, transfering them from hand to hand or to a pocket, in order to keep track of the count. There are various mechanical counting devices, such as golf counters and hand tallies, which may be used. Accurate counting is primarily the product of care and practice.

In order to use pacing as a measure of distance, it is necessary to know the length of the pace or stride. This is determined by pacing over a known distance of several hundred yards. It is wise to pace the same stretch in both directions to minimize errors which might be introduced by a slope or other factor. To determine the length of the pace, divide the known distance paced by the number of paces. For example, if it took 480 paces to cover 1200 ft (200 yd, paced both ways), then the length of pace is 2.5 ft. It would be wise to make several independent determinations, over different courses, before assuming that the natural pace length has been found. If the terrain which is being surveyed is considerably different from that on which the standard pace was measured, another check ought to be run to determine the correct pace length for the new conditions.

If pacing is to be the only method of distance measurement employed, it may be convenient to make and use a pace-scale. The scale can either be in a form suited to the scale of the map or it can convert paces into feet.

Pacing accuracy is admittedly variable, depending on the conditions of the survey and of the pacer. However, it has a fairly low potential error. Good pacing, under favorable conditions, should have an error not in excess of one percent (one part in a hundred). One could easily make an error of the same magnitude through the use of a short tape. Imagine, if you will, the possibilities for error in measuring 100 yd with a 6-ft tape, or a half-mile with a 50-ft tape, each of which would have to be laid down approximately fifty times. So, skill at pacing might be worth cultivating if you want to travel light.

The pedometer is a device for measuring distance, based ultimately upon the pace. It consists of a spring-loaded weight which jounces with each step taken by a person wearing the pedometer (usually hooked on the belt or in a watch pocket). The arc through which the weight is permitted to move is adjustable according to the pace length of the wearer. The weight, acting through a ratchet, moves a gear train leading to pointers on a dial. Pedometers are usually marked in divisions no smaller than a quarter-mile. They are only useful for measuring distances of several miles or more. The price of pedometers ranges from $5 to $10 and they make a dubious investment for the amateur surveyor.

If you have a distance to measure which is sufficient to warrant a pedometer, you may wish to try another gadget. A cyclometer (odometer), which reads in miles and tenths or kilometers and tenths, can be mounted with a single bicycle wheel. Because the cyclometer actually counts revolutions of the wheel, which it converts to distance, it must be of a model adapted to the wheel in use. Cyclometers come to fit wheel diameters from 20 to 28 in. In many parts of the world you will be able to secure the necessary parts from a bicycle dealer or repairman. He may even be prevailed upon to make your long distance measurer. The wheel-cyclometer combination will not work in excessively rough terrain, but it does not require a road. In the long run it will have greater accuracy than the pedometer. In service on bicycles the cyclometer seems to have only a few percent error.

Lately there have appeared on the market several small range finders costing $20 to $45. They have claimed accuracies of two to three percent. Compare with pacing accuracy, but remember the convenience. Some range finders require that you know the size of the target in order to measure the distance. Others, with a more limited range, operate solely on a stereoscopic basis without regard for target

√size. A range finder might be useful where the terrain prohibits direct measurement, possibly across a canyon or a river. However, there are other ways (without knowledge of target size) to make such measurements at no extra cost in instruments. It would seem that the range finders do not add enough to the amateur surveyor's capabilities to warrant the cost.

Even though the telescopic alidade is out of our class, it may be instructive to devote some time to its use in distance measurement. The principles involved are important to us. There are other instruments, such as some surveyor's hand levels, which are equipped with stadia hairs for the same purpose. Even though you never use an alidade you may have access to these levels or wish to improvise something like them.

The alidade's telescope has a series of fine lines ("stadia hairs," "stadia lines") marked on its diaphragm (also "reticle" or "reticule"). The basic vertical and horizontal lines are used for directional and level sighting, respectively. Above and below the horizontal base line are a pair, or two pairs, of other horizontal lines. These outer lines are so spaced that lines of sight past them, above and below the principal (level) line, will intercept a known segment of the stadia rod at a known distance. The stadia rods differ from leveling rods in the following ways: they are often wider, usually have folding rather than sliding sections, are more boldly marked, often with geometric patterns instead of lines, and are less frequently marked with numerals. The stadia rods are designed to be read at greater distances than are the leveling rods. Incidentally, range poles are usually marked with alternate colors at 1 ft intervals (50 centimeters for metric poles) and can be used for rough distance approximations.

Stadia hairs are commonly set, in alidades, in a ratio of 1 to 100. This means that the intercepted length of rod will be 1 ft for each 100 ft of distance. (Simple sighting instruments, like levels, if equipped with stadia hairs usually use a 1:10 ratio instead.) In practice the system works as follows: the uppermost line might cut the 7.4-ft mark on the rod, the middle (level) line cut the 5.8-ft mark, and the lowest line the 4.2-ft mark. The instrument man would interpret this reading in the following fashion. First of all, the point on which the rod rests is 5.8 ft below the instrument. Second, the rod is 320 ft from the instrument (7.4 − 4.2 = 3.2; at 100 ft per foot of rod, 3.2 ft equals 320 ft of distance). It should also be noted that the instrument man, in aiming the alidade, has established the direction of the target. So he marks his ray, measures off the distance, and notes the elevation. This is what makes fancy instrumentation attractive, but you can do as much in other, albeit more laborious, ways.

If we do not plan to use the telescopic alidade, and we do not, then why should we be concerned with all of this? Simply because of the principles involved. Use is made of the principle of proportional triangles, a principle which we can use to great advantage. The instrument is made so that the little triangle formed by the two lines of sight, above and below the level line, and closed at the far end by the plane of the reticle, is proportional to the larger triangle formed by these same sight lines extended to the stadia rod and closed, in effect, by the rod itself. In reality, you would find that the true distance between the stadia hairs is 1 percent of the distance between the eyepiece and the reticle. (See Fig. 25.)

You may wish to try your hand at improvising or modifying instruments to take stadia readings. It was suggested that a homemade alidade might incorporate a telescopic gunsight. If such were the case, it might be possible to modify the gunsight's reticle to work in the same fashion as the alidade's reticle. This calls for skill and precision, but is not impossible. On a simpler scale it ought to be possible to install auxiliary sighting wires or hairs on an open-sight alidade and use them for the same purpose. Because it is difficult to achieve precision spacing of these hairs, another approach will have to be used. With the hairs installed, the instrument would be standardized by noting the intercepts at gradually increasing known distances, for example, 20, 40, 60, 80, and 100 ft. A conversion factor (that is, the actual ratio) could be worked out or a table composed for use in the field. It would be as useful as the standard 1:100 ratio and not much slower to calculate.

The tape measure is the most obvious means of direct distance measurement. Commercially available tapes are adequate with regard to accuracy, but are usually marked in feet and inches. Long metric tapes are quite difficult to find and usually must be secured by special order. Surveyor's tapes are regularly marked in feet and tenths or in metric measure; they have an unmarked portion at the beginning as a handhold. The marking pattern on surveyor's tapes is not the same as that of common tapes. The common tape has each foot (meter) divided into smaller units. You hold the end of the tape on one mark and read the distance at the point where the tape crossed the other mark. With a surveyor's tape there is one unit (foot, meter) subdivided, then the zero mark, and marks at unit intervals for the length of the tape. In use, the front end (zero mark) of the tape is held on the first point and the far end brought to its point. If a fractional unit is to be measured, as it commonly is, the tape is shifted slightly until the far point is at an exact unit mark and the fractional amount is read at the front end of the tape. Although this seems slower, and probably is, it has some advantages when you come to making your own tapes.

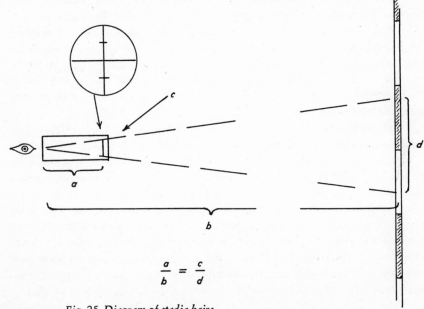

$$\frac{a}{b} = \frac{c}{d}$$

Fig. 25. Diagram of stadia hairs

Common tapes are made of steel, of metallized cloth, and of cloth. Steel tapes are usually to be recommended; they are most commonly available. Metallized cloth tapes have metal threads or wires running along their length to reduce stretching. Plain cloth tapes are just that. Neither metallized tapes nor cloth tapes have much to recommend them unless one needs light weight or the electrically-safe feature of the plain (not metallized!) cloth tape.

If you must have a tape of steel and find the cost high, then consider buying an uncased one. These can be bought either for themselves or as replacements for the ribbons in cased tapes.

For those who must make their own measuring tapes there are a couple of points to bear in mind. String and rope, of whatever kind, are completely unsatisfactory due to their elasticity. Braided forms are worse in this regard than twisted ones. Any substantial metallic strip or ribbon might be used as a tape, if satisfactory markings can be applied. Painted marks do not last very long under field conditions. Interestingly enough, some decorative paper ribbons, of the kind used on gifts, are quite inelastic. They come in spools of 80 ft and are very cheap. The most serious problem with them, as with all paper products, is their instability with humidity changes. Nonetheless, a paper tape is not an impossible expedient. If a wire is used, it should be noted that a solid wire stretches less than a twisted one. A light chain, such as that used on plumbing fixtures or as checkchains on transom windows, might be very usable because it has no stretch. Tags would have to be attached at the marked points.

In making your homemade measuring tape, start with the zero mark about 18 in. from the end, then mark each whole foot on up the tape. (With a metric tape place the zero mark 150 centimeters from the end.) Starting again at the zero mark, and working back toward the starting end of the tape, mark in the subdivisions of your unit. A choice will have to be made between inch marks and tenths-of-a-foot marks; for a metric tape use centimeters and/or decimeters. A professional surveyor calls this style of tape a band chain or a chain tape.

There is no great point in having a tape longer than 100 ft. It is quite clumsy for short measurements unless the excess is housed on a reel. Further, there is some doubt that the crude sighting devices we expect to employ would be workable at the distances warranted by longer tapes—200 to 500 ft. In very rough terrain you may find that a 50-ft tape is all that can be handled due to the necessity of holding it level while measuring.

You might give some thought to using a lightweight staff as an improvised measuring stick. In an area where long canes or bamboo are available, a 16-ft pole with 15 marks at 1-ft intervals and the end section marked in tenths could be very useful. It would be used in the manner of a long yardstick (or meterstick) and has the merit that only one person is needed to handle it.

Finally, remember that a great many elements of a survey are concerned as much with proportions, or relative measures, as they are with absolute measures. This means that you can improvise almost any kind of measuring unit you wish. Your unit of measure might be a stick of arbitrary length. Once back to home base you can measure, in absolute terms, your unit stick and convert your survey into common terms. It may require nothing more than putting a scale on your map.

3

Styles of Surveys

T HERE ARE THREE MAJOR STYLES OF SURVEYS, each appropriate to a set of field conditions and the requirements of the survey. Each has different merits and limitations, calls for more or less skill, and requires more or less instrumentation. It will be up to the surveyor to choose for himself that which he will use. Experience will guide his choices. So will familiarity, and there is no stigma attached to expression of a personal preference. With repeated use of a method there come habituation and mastery, both of which reduce errors.

In addition to outlining the three major styles, several sections will be devoted to four other techniques: the indirect determination of heights; the use of proportional triangles; the technique of offsetting; and the conduct of a leveling traverse. The first three on this list are closely related, as will be seen. Each of these four techniques is not, in itself, a style of surveying, but may contribute to the success and thoroughness of the major styles.

The simplest major style of survey is done with the tape (or chain) alone. It is sometimes called a chain survey. A particular merit of the chain survey is that it is self-checking in the field. Errors are caught at the time of their commission and not at some later date. This survey can be done alone, but is facilitated by one helper to handle the end of the tape. He does not have to be trained in any aspect of surveying to be useful.

The second major style of survey is the compass traverse. For all that a traverse usually progresses in one general direction, the technique can be used in restricted areas. This same technique can be followed, without substantial modification, with a transit or theodolite, but such elaborate instrumentation is hardly consistent with our aim. The principal equipment needed are a compass and a tape. The technique lends itself to one-man operation, but measurements are speeded by having an assistant on the other end of the tape.

The third major survey style is the plane table survey. This can be applied to a discrete area or be conducted as a traverse. Like the chain survey, the plane table method contains elements of self-checking in the field. For plane tabling one needs, minimally, the alidade, the plane table drawing board, and its tripod. If levels are to be run with the survey, then a leveling rod or its equivalent must be added. If distance is to be measured by the use of a stadia rod, then this rod must be added. A leveling rod can serve as a stadia rod and vice versa. Plane tabling, by some approaches, can be done by the surveyor alone. Generally, though, he requires assistance, especially when the leveling or stadia rods are used. The assistant is most helpful when he has some understanding of the plane table method.

Indirect Determination of Heights

Indirect determination of heights may be used to supplement conventional measures of levels. It may be convenient to use the method when the distance is already known, but not the height. It may be necessary to use the method when the point to be measured is not approachable, for example, lies across a stream.

If we know the horizontal distance between our station (the place where a surveyor establishes his instrument) and the target, and the angle of elevation of the target, we may employ a figure, the tangent, which represents the ratio between certain sides of this triangle. (See Fig. 26.) The tangent, in the form of a decimal figure appropriate to the angle of elevation, is multiplied by the horizontal distance (d). The product is the height (h) of the side of the triangle opposite the measured angle.

Tangents, which are formally known as trigonometric functions, are to be found in books of surveying tables, in trigonometry textbooks, and in books of mathematical tables. Though pocket tables are to be found, a field approximation dispenses with tables. The tangent of an angle of 1° is approximately one-sixtieth (1/60). The tangents of other small angles will be approximately the reciprocal of the number obtained by dividing 60 by the number of degrees in the angle. Thus, the tangent of 2° is 1/30; the tangent of 6° is 1/10. This approximation ceases to be valid for angles greater than 10°, which is itself a substantial slope. For greater angles, consult the appropriate tables.

To use this indirect method you must have some method of measuring an angle of elevation or depression. Usually this will be done with a clinometer, but other means can be improvised. For instance, if you were to take a carpenter's level, aim it toward the point to be sighted, set it level, and then measure the lift of the far end, you would have an expedient angle measuring set-up. If, for example, you had a 2 ft-long level and shimmed up the end 2 inches when taking the sight, then the angle sighted is 5°. (In this case you are solving the little triangle under the level.)

d equals 24 in., h equals 2 in.:

$$\frac{d}{h} = \frac{24}{2} = 12$$

$$\text{and} \frac{60}{12} = 5$$

therefore, the angle is 5°. (See Fig. 27.)

Another indirect height measuring method makes use of two known angles. For this reason, even though vertical angles must be sighted, you can improvise a sighting device in advance and do not have to cope, on the spot, with the measurement of unknown angles. If you stand so that the line of sight to the unknown point (target) is 45° elevation, and then back away until the angle is 26½°, the distance between the first station and the second is equal to the height of the target above the instrument level. (See Fig. 28.) The only qualifications are that the two stations must be at the same elevation and lie on a straight line with the target.

In both of these methods, remember to include in your calculations the height of the instrument itself above the ground. It will likely be at eye level, possibly 5 ft high.

In addition to the use of the indirect method to determine heights above the station level, it may be used to determine depressions below the station level. This less frequent application is often overlooked.

If you have a good base map of the region, you might find the indirect method, using tangents, valuable for determining your station elevation above mean

Fig. 26. Tangents for height determination

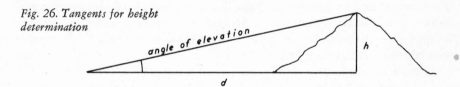

angle of elevation

h

d

Fig. 27. Level to measure vertical angles

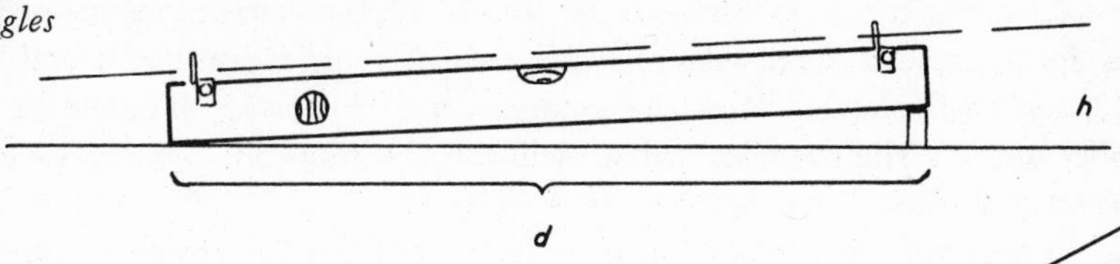

h

d

Fig. 28. Remote measurement of height

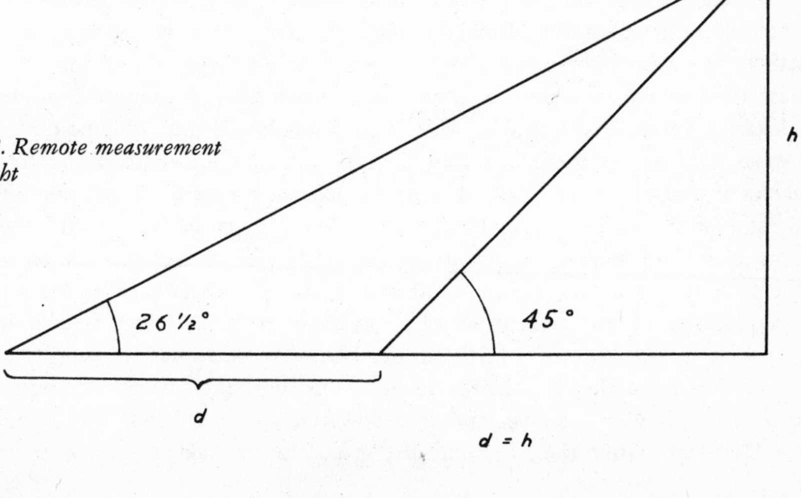

26 ½°

45°

h

d

d = h

sea level. Often major surveys include the elevation of mountain tops when they do not indicate those of lesser landmarks. If you can find such a mountain peak on a government survey map and can locate your own station on the same map, then you can figure your own elevation by subtracting the apparent height of the mountain (taken from your station) from the published elevation figure for it. You must, of course, be able to read from the map the horizontal distance between your station and the mountain top. The same system might be worked, using an angle of depression, if you are on a ridge or slope overlooking a valley where there is a bridge or a railroad line of known elevation. Then you would add the observed depression (that is, "height") to the published elevation to derive that of your station.

Proportional Triangles

Proportional triangles have been introduced before, in the discussion of the stadia hairs in an alidade. In that instance the little triangle formed within the instrument between eyepiece and reticle was proportional to a much larger triangle formed outside the instrument between the eyepiece and the stadia rod. The employment of the principle of proportional triangles enables us to do many things other than design instruments.

There is a circumstance, well known to those who have studied plane geometry, which will help us tremendously in our work. It is this: any triangle whose sides have lengths in the ratios of 3:4:5 is necessarily a right-angled triangle, with the right angle lying opposite the side having a proportional length of 5 and between those having lengths of 3 and 4. The absolute size of the triangle does not matter as long as the ratio between the lengths of the sides is maintained. This means, for example, that the sides of such a triangle could measure 3, 4, and 5 in., or 9, 12, and 15 ft (having used here a multiplier of 3), or 75, 100, and 125 ft (multiplier of 25). The triangles that we will use will probably measure 10 to 20 ft on the shortest side.

The chances are great that we will be laying out triangles using either a 50-ft or 100-ft tape, and with only one tape at hand. For example, in a survey we wish to lay out a line at right angles to our general survey line. (See Fig. 29.) Mark the point of departure, B, with a stake. Then measure along the survey line a distance proportional to the "4" side of the triangle and mark this point, C, with a stake. (In the figure this distance has been taken as either 16 or 32 ft, using factors of 4 or 8, respectively.) Measure out from B a distance proportional to the "3" side of the triangle. (In the example, either 12 or 24 ft.) Finally, measure from point C a distance proportional to the "5" side of the triangle (20 or 40 ft). The place at which the "3" measurement and the "5" measurement come together is the location of the third corner of the triangle, point D, which is then staked. The angle included between lines BC and BD is then a right angle, or 90°.

This measuring procedure can be carried out single-handed or with help. It can be done with a single tape or with several tapes. If alone and using only one 50-ft tape, fasten the front end of the tape to the stake at B, also fasten the

48-ft mark of the tape to this same stake. Then measure off 16 ft on the survey line to establish point C and set a stake. Run the tape around stake C and, holding the 36-ft mark, pull the tape taut from stakes B and C. The stake to mark point D is then driven where the 36-ft mark comes to rest. If you use a 100-ft tape, then your points are 0, 96 ft, 32 ft, and 72 ft, respectively. This method will work, although it is hard on steel tapes and the stakes themselves, being inside the triangle, are a source of small error.

The tape loop method is best suited to single-handed work and makes the largest triangles possible when running a 50-ft or 100-ft tape around the entire triangle.

Another method, using a single tape, is to hold the dead end of the tape at B and mark an arc on the ground, as though you were using compasses, with a stake's point. The stake is held at the proper distance along the tape and the mark scratched about where you think point D will fall. Then move the tape to point C and repeat the process, using the proper measurement. The intersection of the two arcs is the point D. If you have two tapes, fasten the dead end of one at B and the dead end of the other at C. Then tighten the tapes, holding on to your distance points on the tapes. The place where the distance points meet, with the tapes taut, is the point D. Because the arc-swinging method doesn't require the tape to encircle the triangle, the measurements may be larger, if desired, than those used in the tape loop method up to the limits of tape length. The maximum lengths of sides, with a 100-ft tape, would be 60, 80, and 100 ft.

The proportions which smaller triangles bear to larger ones, or vice versa, can be useful. The application of these proportional triangles makes maneuvering in a limited space much more feasible. Offsetting, by contrast, usually involves the layout of triangles which are, so to speak, life-size.

An application of proportional smaller and larger triangles is to be seen in the following indirect measurement of distance.

Suppose, in the situation shown in Fig. 30, that you can reach point C, but are unable to reach point D to measure the distance CD. Starting at point C you establish the line AC at right angles to the line CD. The distance to A is arbitrary, the only requirement being that point D must be visible from point A. Once point A is set, you establish point B at a convenient point on the line AC. From point B you set off a right angle to point C, which must lie on the line AD. Then you measure the distances AB, BE, and AC. The distance CD is your unknown quantity. (In the figure some simple figures are shown; you will not be so lucky!) The relationship between the dimensions of the two triangles can be expressed in a formula in which one then substitutes the measured values:

$$\frac{AB}{BE} = \frac{AC}{CD} \text{ or } \frac{10}{5} = \frac{100}{CD} \text{ or } 10\,CD = 500 \text{ or } CD = 50$$

To solve an equation like this, which is simple algebra, all you do is cross multiply, then divide by the number associated with your unknown (CD in this instance). There might be occasions on which you would want to solve for another unknown, such as the distance BE. Only one of the four figures can be unknown at a time.

This same method can be used to determine unknown heights, as of a cliff. Simply visualize the triangles turned on edge and sight from the ground across the top of a known height to the top of the cliff. Measure the distances from your eye to the base of the rod and the base of the cliff. Substitute in the equation and solve for the unknown.

Offsetting

If the world's surface were as flat and unobstructed as a billiard table, there would be no need for offsetting. However, in virtually every survey there comes an occasion when one wishes to establish a line parallel to the general survey line, or to dodge around an obstacle, or to locate a point lying to one side of the survey line. Offsetting can meet these and other needs.

The layout of a right-angled triangle, as mentioned in the section on proportional triangles, is the basis for one type of offsetting. With this layout one can establish a line parallel to the original survey line. This shift may be desirable when

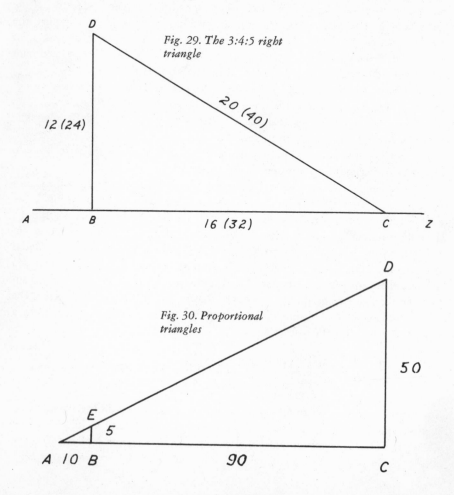

Fig. 29. The 3:4:5 right triangle

12 (24)

20 (40)

A   B   16 (32)   C   Z

Fig. 30. Proportional triangles

D

50

E
5

A 10 B   90   C

one finds the survey line, as in a traverse, working onto a rough slope or into another undesirable situation. One proceeds to layout the right-angle triangle as described before. Then the line BD, at right angles to the survey line, is carried out to twice its original length. The hypotenuse of the triangle, line CD, is also carried out to twice its original length. The terminal points of these lines, E and F, respectively, mark a line parallel to the original base line, AZ, or more specifically BC. (See Fig. 31.)

In the example, the offset produced is based on the use of a 50-ft tape at its maximum to establish the first triangle, BCD. This gives a distance from B to D of 30 ft and an offset of 60 ft. A larger offset can be obtained if the line extensions beyond point D are greater than 30 and 50 ft, respectively. If this is done the sides of triangle DEF must be in the original 3:4:5 proportions; one simple way to retain the proper proportions would be to double or treble the measurements of the sample. Thus, one would have triangle DEF with sides of 60, 80, and 100 ft, or sides of 90, 120, and 150 ft. A major consideration is that, whatever the gross size, the lines BDE and CDF must be kept straight.

If you are using offsetting to step around an obstacle on the general survey line, then the procedure just outlined is followed. One pursues the alternate (parallel) survey line until the obstacle is passed and then offsets back by the same distance. You are now on the same line as your original survey.

One merit of this mode of offsetting is that measurement of forward progress, along the survey lines, is not upset. Having worked one's way along to point B, one simply continues from point E toward point F and beyond. The type of offset which will next be considered lacks this feature. The line is paralleled, but the distance measure is not necessarily transferred.

The same sort of offsetting which can be done with right-angle triangles may also be done with triangles of other shapes. Starting from the survey line at point A, lay off a straight line, angling away from the survey line. (See Fig. 32.) Continue this line so that the distances AC and CD are equal; mark the three points. Starting at point B, which is any other point along the original survey line, run a line out to C and then continue it to point E. The line must be straight and the distances BC and CE must be equal, but not necessarily equal to AC and CD. The line connecting points D and E is parallel to the original survey line, AB.

It will be observed that the distances AB and DE are equal. This technique can, consequently, be used to measure distances by offset. However, remember that forward progress in the direction of the original survey cannot be measured accurately if you stop one measuring process at point B, for example, and resume the measurement at point D.

Much the same kind of approach can give a reversed offset to measure distance indirectly. This is shown in Figure 33 and involves the use of right-angle triangles. Suppose that you wish to measure the distance between A and B, on opposite sides of a river or a ravine. At point A set out a line at right angles to the line of sight across the river. At a suitable distance along this line mark point C with an obvious marker and continue an equal distance along the same line to D. AC and CD must be equal distances. Lay out another right angle, running back from point D, giving you a line parallel to the original line of sight. This will take

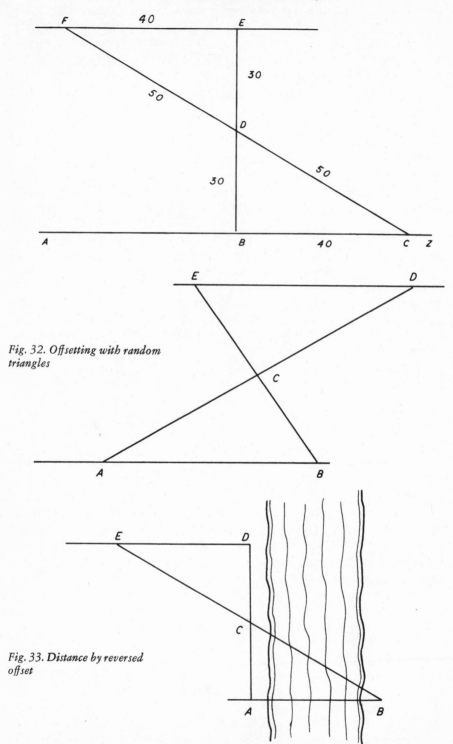

Fig. 31. Offsetting with right triangles

Fig. 32. Offsetting with random triangles

Fig. 33. Distance by reversed offset

you in the direction of point E, which is not yet determined. Continue from D away from the river until a sight from your position finds that the marker at C lines up with the target at point B. This point is then determined as point E. The distance DE will be the same as the distance AB which is the one for which you are solving the problem.

Obviously the above reversed offset has some limits if the distance from A to B is great, because the distance from D to E must be just the same. A technique using proportional triangles will enable you to reduce the distance on the ground.

Offsetting is the regular method of dealing with points which lie to the side of the main survey line. The survey line is kept as straight as possible in order to minimize angular errors. The alternative would be to have the survey line "snake" along, going from one feature to another which was to be mapped. (See Figs. 34a and 34b.) The sources of error in such a procedure are many and it is to be avoided.

Instead, the survey line is set to pass through areas of interest. Then offsets are measured from this line to the particular points with which one is concerned. The offset lines are usually at right angles to the main survey line; the angle is judged by eye, swung as a compass bearing, noted with the angle prism, or laid off with a 3:4:5 triangle. Of these methods the eye, the compass, and the angle prism are the quickest and the easiest to use. Among other things, one does not have to make such an accurate initial guess on the location of the point from which the initial departure is taken.

Having set off the line at right angles and leading to the point in question, one measures along that line to determine the distance between the survey line and the target. It is just that simple a procedure. (See Fig. 35.)

As a final note on this subject we may add yet another way of setting up a right angle across the survey line. It requires more maneuvering room than the 3:4:5 triangle, but it is quicker. From a point on the survey line swing an arc, using as your radius a tape or other inelastic item. Scribe a short arc on either side of the main line. Move along the survey line to another point, more distant than the radius of the first arc, and swing a second arc so that portions of it intersect the scribed lines of the first arc. Scribe in these intersecting segments. A line which passes through the two points of intersection will lie across the main survey line at right angles. The radii of the two arcs do not have to be equal, but they usually are so measured. Importantly, there are no absolute measurements involved so this can be done with the crudest of field equipment.

The Leveling Traverse

A leveling traverse may serve two purposes, separately or simultaneously. It may be used to "carry" a level from a known point, such as an established bench mark, to some point in your survey area, such as a prime surveying station. Or the traverse may establish the elevation of a series of points along its line, which will likely be that of the main survey.

Leveling calls for a minimal complement of equipment. You must have a device for level sighting and some type of leveling rod. Items in both categories have already been discussed in the section on equipment and expedient substitutes.

Any leveling instrument, especially a homemade one, is subject to error. There is nothing wrong with an error as long as the amount and the direction of it are known and are consistent. We can always apply the known correction to determine the true reading or adjust the instrument to read correctly. The instrument properly applied can be used to check itself.

The consistent, or built-in, error of an instrument, whether it is a complex instrument or as simple as a tape measure, is known as the "index error." The

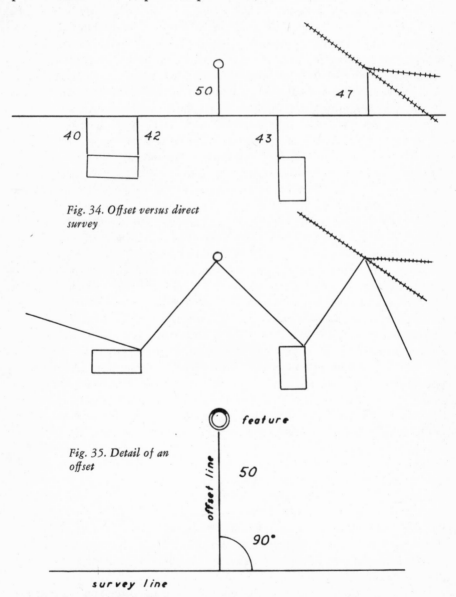

Fig. 34. Offset versus direct survey

Fig. 35. Detail of an offset

feature

offset line

50

90°

survey line

simplest way to determine the index error of a leveling instrument is by the reciprocal sights method. In this method the instrument is used to check itself and no comparative standard is needed. This is quite valuable in the field when a just-completed expedient instrument can immediately be checked.

Starting with two stations, such as the tops of fence posts, about 50 yd apart, the instrument is rested on each in turn and sighted at the other. If the instrument is true, the two readings—one of elevation and one of depression—will be the same number of degrees. Under most circumstances some index error will be observed. The true reading will be the average of the two reciprocal readings. For example, the reading from station one to station two is 16° depression, while the reverse reading is 12° elevation. Therefore the true reading is 14° and the index error of the instrument is $-2°$. If the instrument is adjustable an effort may be made to remove the error by adjustment (with subsequent rechecking) or you may apply the index error to each reading taken.

The technique above applies to instruments which measure angles of elevation or depression, such as clinometers. A variant technique, still employing reciprocal sights, must be used to check and correct instruments which only indicate level lines, such as hand levels. Again two stations are used, each sighting at the other. Sight from station one to station two and mark where the level sightline strikes station two. Then take a reciprocal, or "back-" sight from the height of this mark to the original location of the instrument at station one. If the reciprocal sight strikes the original instrument level at station one, then the instrument is accurate. If the second sightline strikes high, the instrument reads high by half of the increase. Or the error may be the other way (downward) and again the error is half of the observed displacement of the second sightline.

Though you now have a measurement of the instrument error, it still has to be converted to a usable index error figure. For example, you may have found that your reciprocal sight fell low by 0.4 ft. The displacement, measured in this fashion, is dependent upon the distance. So your observed displacement of 0.4 ft is halved to get 0.2 ft and stated as 0.2 ft at the distance, say 150 ft, which station two is removed from station one. So your sight is down 0.13 ft per 100 ft of distance. This is your usable index error. If you are unable to adjust the instrument to produce a zero index error, then you apply the foregoing figure to each sight taken.

Once you have established the accuracy or the index error of your equipment, you are prepared to commence the leveling traverse itself. It might seem simplest to carry a leveling traverse by taking a sight from instrument to rod, then moving the instrument to that rod station, advancing the rod, and repeating the process. Logically, this is the easiest way, but it is also the easiest way to incorporate in your work a constantly accumulating error. If, for example, the instrument should have an unaccounted error of 0.1 ft in 100 ft (which is only 0.1 percent error) you would accumulate 2.64 ft of error in a half mile.

A system of reciprocal sights for the traverse will prevent the accumulation of error. You start off with a back sight. The rod is set up on the starting point (station one, zero distance) which is probably a bench mark or your base station. The instrument is established on the line of the traverse in the direction of travel. A sight is taken and recorded. The distance from station one to the instrument is measured. The rodman then moves along the line of traverse ahead of the instrument a distance equal to that from station one to the instrument. This may mean that the rodman paces along the survey line, counting, until he reaches the instrument. Here he restarts his count and continues until he reaches the same count. Here he stops and sets his rod at what is now station two. A second sight, forward along the survey line, is taken and recorded. The instrument is then moved ahead of the rod any convenient distance and the procedure repeated. It should be noted that the instrument is turned to take the back- and foresights, so that the sighting is always done with the eye at the same end of the instrument. (In some cases the nature of the instrument guarantees that this is done.) If you sight through alternate ends of the instrument, assuming it is possible, then you will defeat the purpose of the system. Also note that the distance from the instrument to the rod for each pair of sights, the backsight and the foresight, must be equal, though the amount is discretionary. The difference in observed elevation between the two rod stations is the difference between the two readings. (See Fig. 36 for a leveling diagram and a mode of recording.)

The manner of recording provides a check on the arithmetic of the surveyor. The difference between the sum of the backsights and the sum of the foresights should equal the difference in level between the first and the last stations of the traverse. If the two figures are not equal, there must be an error of calculation or observation or recording, not an instrument error.

With this recording scheme only the amounts of the backsights and foresights need to be recorded in the field. The rest can be calculated later, but doing so will forfeit an immediate check on one's operations. Note that the backsight and foresight for each rod station are recorded on the line for that station. This makes the recording progression on the sheet move from a backsight on one line to a foresight on the next line, then to a backsight on the same line, and so on. At first glance this may be confusing, but a moment's comparison of the diagram and the recording system will make it clearer.

The distances or locations of the rod may not be vital if the traverse is only concerned with the end stations. (Subject to the necessity of having the rod distance the same figure for each pair of sights from an instrument location.) The distances noted are those between rod stations. If the traverse is to gain a profile and the line is not straight, then the directions must also be recorded. The directions of the rod from the instrument for each pair of sights do not have to be 180° apart (that is, on a straight line), but the rod stations must be equidistant from the instrument. (See Fig. 37.) It may even be necessary, because of terrain problems, to place the instrument to one side of the traverse line, but in such cases the equal distance rule must be observed.

Contours

Maps of the type with which we are primarily concerned customarily indicate vertical as well as horizontal spatial relationships. The archeologist's interest in vertical spacing is well known and requires no further comment. It would be well for other investigators to be sensitive to the role which may be played by vertical space. Housing patterns, the locations of industrial sites, the routes of communication, and the siting of temples may all be closely correlated with elevation. Consequently one can hardly consider a survey to be thorough without having taken account of this factor.

Fig. 36. Leveling traverse and recording diagram

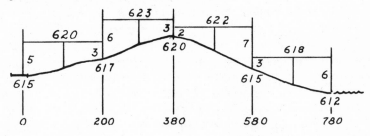

Back-sight	Fore-sight	Instru-ment	Ground	Dis-tance	Notes
5		620	615	0	Road
6	3	623	617	200	
2	3	622	620	380	Top of dune
3	7	618	615	580	
	6		612	780	Lake
16	19		3		

Fig. 37. Leveling traverses: straight versus sinuous

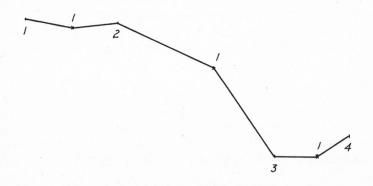

The leveling traverse will provide the needed data for spot elevations. It may also be used to link, in terms of elevation, the several stations of a survey. However, extensive mapping of elevations for contours will probably employ other, quicker methods which are less precise.

Elevations are usually shown on maps in two ways: either the elevations of certain key locations are shown in numerical notation or a series of lines are drawn to join points of equal elevation. Additionally, elevation differences are sometimes shown by shading, color, or hatching, but this is an aspect of drafting and will not be discussed here. Our first concern is with the derivation of data.

The surveying of spot elevations is comparatively easy and readily displayed on your map. Such places as the survey stations must be shown. To these you may wish to add the elevation of a plaza, dance ground, canoe house, temple, chief's house, grist mill, and so forth. If your work stresses problems of communication you may want to note the elevation of mountain passes, the distance down to the beach, or the drop of a river. There will be a finite number of points, determined by their significance to your study and the available time.

The lines which join points of equal elevation are called contour lines, or briefly "contours." The contour is the line of intersection of an imaginary horizontal plane with the surface of the ground. It may be most simply visualized if you consider the following illustration. If you took a half potato and set it, cut side down, on a table surface, then sliced through it parallel to the table surface, the cut edges would mark the contours of that vegetable. An important characteristic of contours is that any one contour line ultimately forms a loop. The loop of the topmost contour on the potato will be quite small; the loop of the lowest potato contour will be comparatively larger. The same holds in most circumstances on the land—the higher, the smaller the loop.

Further, contour lines are roughly parallel to each other. Differences in parallelism arise when there is a change in the angle of a slope; at these points the lines will diverge or converge for a distance. The horizontal spacing of contour lines offers a clue to the degree of slope. Their vertical spacing remains constant on a given map. Given the vertical spacing, the gentle slope will have widely spaced contours and the steep slope closely spaced contours. Contour lines do not normally cross each other. The qualification "normally" is added here because someone is always quick to point out that contour lines can cross where there exists an overhanging cliff. So, if you find such a cliff, be sure to cross your contours!

Contour lines are spaced vertically by a distance appropriate to the map scale, the ruggedness of the terrain, and the purposes for which the survey is conducted. This vertical spacing is called the contour interval and varies in United States practice from 200-ft intervals to intervals of less than 1 ft. The larger contour intervals are used where the terrain is mountainous and the population sparse or in cases where a generalized overview is intended. For example, the U.S. Geological Survey's topographic map of Yosemite National Park is at a scale of 1:125000 (about ½ in. to the mile) and a contour interval of 100 ft. The Western United States 1:250000 series (about ¼ in. to the mile) uses a 200-ft contour interval with supplementary 100-ft contours on some maps, and the World Aeronautical Chart series, at 1:1000000 scale, has contours at 1000-ft intervals. At the other end of the scale one finds common U.S. Geological Survey topographic maps with 20-ft contours and special maps for land leveling (for irrigation) at intervals of less than 1 ft.

It may sound as though the determination and drawing of contour lines would be a virtually endless process. This would, indeed, be the case if short cuts were not taken. One does not check, by leveling, every point along every contour. In practice, the surveyor records the elevation of a series of check points on the terrain and then sketches in, by eye, the lines joining points of equal elevation. The choice of check points requires some skill. One should favor those places which show maximum relief such as points along the spur from a ridge as well as points in the flanking ravines. Basically, the greatest difference between spot eleva-tion and the contour system lies in the drawing of the contour lines.

There is no rule by which one may determine the proper contour interval to employ. Keep in mind that the smaller the interval the greater the labor in surveying; you will have to use more check points and there will be more sketch-ing. Consider, when setting the interval, what is likely to be a significant difference in elevation. This may be coordinated with the general relief of the area. A few feet may be very important in a flat or swampy area and insignificant alongside a 10,000-ft mountain.

The ability to plot your results on the map will place some limitations on contour intervals. If the interval is small and the slope is great, it may be impos-sible to plot the contours as distinctly separate lines. This circumstance would call for modification of plans for scale or for contour interval.

You may calculate, in advance, the plotted spacing of contours at a given interval with terrain slopes of a given angle. In the section on indirect height measurement we made use of tangents to solve a triangle of known length, but unknown height. The formula employed was:

$$\text{height} = \text{tangent} \times \text{horizontal distance}$$

In this case we have a known height, but an unknown distance. The formula is altered to read:

$$\text{horizontal distance} = \frac{\text{contour interval}}{\text{tangent}}$$

To put this formula into use, assume that the contour interval is 20 ft and that the angle of the slope is 25°. The tangent of 25° is 0.4663 (from a table of natural tangents). Substituting, we get:

$$\text{horizontal distance} = \frac{20}{0.4663}$$

or

$$\text{horizontal distance} = 42.89 \text{ ft}$$

If the scale of the map were 1:24000 (or 1 in. to 2000 ft), then 42.89 ft would scale at slightly over 0.02 in. on the map. This would be virtually impossible as a working spacing and some other arrangement of contour interval or scale would be in order.

Contour lines are often designated by their elevation: for example, "the 640-ft contour." This terminology arises partially from the manner in which contours are labelled. Usually the elevation number (in feet or meters) is written into a short break in the line so that the numbers read along the general trend of the line. Not every contour is so marked; marking is often limited to every fifth contour. Thus, with a 100-ft interval, the numbers are found at the 500-ft and 1000-ft contours. One can readily count up or down a few lines to the contour in question. To label more contours would result in a severe cluttering of the map.

The Chain Survey

The chain, or tape, survey is made using only one piece of field equipment—the measuring tape. In these terms it is by far the simplest method, yet can produce satisfactory results. The use of other equipment would not enhance its accuracy, but only the speed with which the area might be covered.

This style of survey can be conducted to make forward progress along a line, not necessarily straight, but it is an arduous process. One would employ straight-line measurements exclusively and combine them with techniques of off-setting and the use of proportional and other triangles to establish the angles at necessary turns. (See Fig. 38.) While this application of the chain survey is something of a tour de force, it may be necessitated by circumstances. The point is that it can be done.

More usually the chain survey style is applied to a discrete, usually compact, area and the features within it. You commence by regularizing the outlines of the area. A series of straight lines are struck off along the perimeter of the area. Do this using as few lines as possible and endeavor to set each line so that it "averages" the direction of the area boundary which it parallels. Some portions of the area will fall inside your lines; other portions will fall outside. If possible keep these areas approximately equal. This regularizing process is done on a preliminary sketch of the area. (See Fig. 39.)

You start your survey, if possible, at one end of the longest straight line determined in the preliminary sketch. On a regular area, use the longest real side. Mark each end with a stake and measure the length of this line. Make a note on your preliminary sketch, and proceed around the perimeter of your area, setting a stake at each corner and measuring each line. All measurements are noted on the preliminary sketch.

Now you have determined distances, but not directions. It may be seen that the figure outlined could be "warped" by changing the angles without changing the perimeter distance so that it could enclose more or less area. Therefore, you need to stabilize the figure by measuring some internal distances. On this area, as diagrammed, three cross-measurements will suffice. You measure from A to E, from B to E, and from B to D. Note the distances on your sketch. You have now measured the sides of four triangles—AFE, ABE, BED, and BCD. Remember that when the lengths of all three sides of a triangle are determined, its shape is known. One cannot vary any of the angles without changing the length of one or more sides.

To plot the results of your survey, you first draw a line scaled for the distance AB. This line can be used as a base line to which all other lines are referred. Then lay off two arcs, from A and B, which will cross at point E. The radius in each case will be the properly scaled distance taken from your notes and preliminary sketch. Then lay off the distances from A to F and from E to F, each properly scaled. The intersection of the two arcs will determine the location of point F. Next lay off, as arcs, the measured distances from B to C and from D to C; their intersection will set point C. You now have established the outlines, in regularized form, of your area. (See Fig. 40.)

Having determined the perimeter of your area, you can be concerned with the details of the boundary. It may be sufficient to sketch in, by eye, the actual borders using the survey lines (AB, BC, CD, and so on) for guidance. If this is not precise enough for your purposes, then run a series of offsets from the regularized perimeter to points on the real boundary.

Details within the general outline are handled in much the same way as the outline itself. Measurements to these details are made from the corner stakes

Fig. 38. A sinuous chain traverse

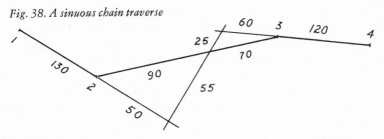

Fig. 39. Regularizing the survey area

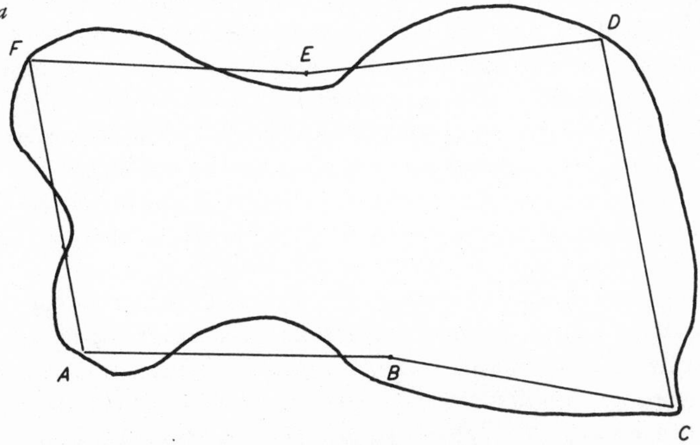

or they can be located by means of offsets from the perimeter lines. If the tape alone is being used, it will probably be easier to measure the distances from corners, as there are fewer tape maneuvers than are involved in setting up right angles for the offsets. If, on the other hand, you have an angle prism or equivalent available, the offsets can be quickly located and measured. Note that the measurements from the corners will be used in plotting as radii of arcs swung from these corners. The intersections of the arcs are the locations of the features.

Some comment on arc intersections might be in order at this juncture. The basis for the use of this method is called triangulation, the circumstance being that you are measuring from the ends of one side of a triangle to the vertex opposite. The sharpest intersection of these arcs occurs when they meet at the highest possible angle, a right angle (if this can be applied to the meeting of curves) being ideal. At any lower angle there will be a longer zone of overlap of the intersection and greater uncertainty about the location. Control of the arc intersection is gained through planning of the triangle you temporarily establish when measuring for the arcs. If the centers of the arcs lie about as far apart as the distance from either of them to the unknown point, then you achieve the ideal angle by forming an equilateral triangle.

Be a bit cautious about the lengths of your offsets in this style of work. If you are working with the simplest of tools, then you may be determining the right angle for offset by eye. There is no reason why you should not do so in the interests of speed and simplicity. However, a small error in the angle can produce a large variation at a distance. For example, a 5° error in judging the angle can produce an 8.8-ft lateral difference at a distance of only 100 ft. Observe that the major difference will occur laterally. You know that the point is somewhere on the arc of distance from the point of offset, but you will not know precisely where. If the distance is more important than the direction, then perhaps you can find the possible error supportable. Otherwise, use shorter offset lines.

In dealing with the chain survey of this limited area, we have followed the approach of measuring the perimeter (or a regularized version of it) and then stabilizing the results with a series of tie lines across the area. It is possible to accomplish the same result by working from a single straight survey line on which are constructed a series of appropriate triangles. Offsets may be run from this line or from other lines of the survey. The survey line is usually set to have the maximum possible length across the area. Its extremities are usually at the limits of the area. With proper planning, for which time should be allowed, it is possible to have great economy of effort. The lines which are measured serve not only to set corners or other perimeter features, but also are the basis for subsidiary triangles and offsets for individual features within the area. (See Fig. 41 for the same area as in Fig. 40, now surveyed in this alternative style.)

Although the lengths of three sides fix a triangle, there is no inherent check on the accuracy of these sides unless some sides are shared by triangles. Errors in one part, in this shared instance, will be reflected in the failure of the whole to work out properly when drawing the map. It is small comfort to have found an error at this late stage when one has no idea of its location. A field measurement may be taken which will not give an immediate check on accuracy, but will give checks on individual triangles during plotting of results. A measurement across a triangle between two known points on any two sides is your check. If the whole triangle has been properly measured, recorded, and plotted, then this measurement will fit at the scale chosen. If it does not fit you had better see what is in error. A single check line may be carried straight across two or more triangles; it can have the auxiliary function of locating subsidiary points or as a base for offsets. Careful planning is essential for prevention of wasted motion.

The chain survey is unquestionably the simplest method of surveying an area. It does not even require the use of a chain (measuring tape) if you are content to pace the distances. The accuracy may be quite adequate for your purposes and it provides a planned, organized way in which to make a record. Every field worker ought to understand this style of survey because it can be practiced anywhere at any time without premeditation.

Fig. 40. Triangulation of the survey area

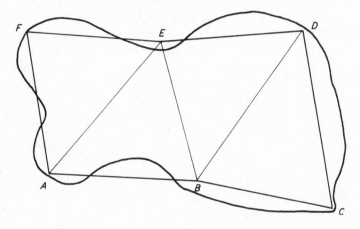

Fig. 41. Chain survey line with subsidiary triangles

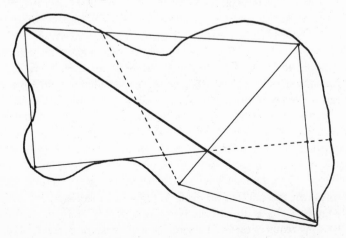

The Compass Traverse

The compass traverse proceeds by measured angles and distances. It is the basic style pursued by most professional surveyors in their work. In addition to the same equipment used to measure distances for the chain survey, one must have some means of measuring horizontal angles and directions. The compass provides the means in this instance.

There are two different compass traverses: the closed traverse in which the survey line comes back to its starting place, and the open traverse in which the survey line does not return to its starting place. The closed traverse has built into it the means of checking the accuracy of the survey; the open traverse must rely on other information for such a verification.

The first move in a compass traverse is to mark your first station, then the second station. The line between the two stations on a traverse is called a leg. A compass bearing is taken from the first station to the second. The length of the leg is measured, and offsets are taken at points along the leg in order to locate the individual features desired. From the second station the surveyor takes a back bearing to station one. It should be exactly 180° different from the forward bearing. It probably will not be exactly this figure. If the difference is small, only a few degrees, the surveyor will take the average of the two bearings (the observed bearing and the expected bearing) as his figure. If the discrepancy is large, then he must seek out the cause and take steps to correct it. He may have encountered a local magnetic anomaly (railroad track, steel bridge, metal fence) for which the "cure" is to move to a location along the survey line more distant from the disturbance.

If a leveling traverse is planned it can be combined with the compass traverse. Remember that the leveling rod, which might be used for a compass sighting target, goes on each station while the instrument goes at the midpoint between. Backsighting is a part of the procedure for both purposes so there is little extra effort involved in the incorporation of the other type of traverse.

The compass traverse continues in this fashion with each station being selected for its significance in the overall survey plan. Eventually in the closed traverse you will come back to the starting point as your final station. Be sure to make that final sight and level determination. If you do not take the sight to close the circuit, you will forfeit the self-checking feature of the closed traverse. In the open traverse you will arrive at your last station. If possible you will have selected for this ultimate station some point which is known on another basis. It may appear on a government survey, or you may have located it by an independent survey in which you place faith. The final point on your traverse as planned may not be such a spot, but extension of the traverse to include such a place will be rewarding as a check on your accuracy.

Booking, or recording, of your survey has to be done carefully because it is usually not drawn to scale in the field. A simplified method of booking is to draw a preliminary field sketch with the bearings, distances, and levels noted on it. (See Fig. 42.) This requires care to be sure that one measure is not confused with another—that is, that you do not take as the bearing a number which is a distance.

A columnar mode is basically a three-column system (four if you include levels) with one column for bearings, one for distance on the main survey line, and one for notes. Each line across pertains to one event—a station, an offset, a feature—and has the appropriate numbers on it. Generally it will suffice to write in the name of the event, but occasionally words will fail you and a small sketch may be clearer. The merit of columnar separation is that there is no chance of confusing one measure with another.

Individuals who are concerned about instrument accuracy, who struggle to make careful measurements in a thicket, and who remeasure for assurance, are often those whose notation systems fall far short of the same standards. The best advice is to record as though the plotting were to be done by someone who had never seen the area. It is possible that this may happen and skimpy or messy notation will take its toll.

Before we turn to the plotting of a compass traverse, we might consider one interesting aspect of a compass traverse contrasted with a theodolite or transit traverse. The compass does not have reading accuracy much finer than 1° and possibly more. The transit may read to a minute or less of arc. The technique with the transit is to start with an initial orientation and measure the angles which the legs of the traverse bear to each other, each successive leg being related to the one preceding. If an error is introduced in any leg, or consistently in each leg, it will be magnified in subsequent steps. The errors are cumulative. On the other hand, the compass bearing is always referred back to the magnetic field (or magnetic north, if you wish), not to a previous bearing. Therefore the error of one measurement is not magnified by subsequent measurements. If an error gets into the works, it stays but does not grow in magnitude.

Once the compass traverse has been completed, one makes a trial plot. Using a sheet of graph paper as a convenient base, the distances and angles are laid off. It may be found that the figure fails to close as the last leg of a closed traverse is plotted. That is, the terminal point of the last plotted leg does not fall on the starting point of the first leg. In some cases it is possible to ignore this "error of closure," if the amount is insignificant in view of the nature of the survey. (This is one instance where having the surveyor and the user of the survey one and the same person has its advantages. You do not find the surveyor striving for unnecessary precision nor failing to provide it when needed.) More usually, you will wish to make a correction of the trial figure.

The error of closure may come from a gradual accumulation of minor errors of measurement. Most of them are presumably randomly distributed and cancel each other out, but there will be a residual error. Because one does not know specifically where the error came from, it is necessary to distribute the error proportionally back along the survey line. The easiest way to handle this is graphically, although it can be calculated.

In this correction for the error of closure, both distance and direction are corrected on the assumption that errors will occur in both. First you note, on your plot, a line which makes that closure, from the end of the final leg to the initial station. Then through each station en route you rule a line parallel to the line on the error of closure. To distribute the error proportionally, you scale off a line equal to the length of the traverse. (You may have to do this in segments.) At appropriately scaled points for each station you erect a perpendicular to the line. The perpendicular for the last station is scaled in length to equal the error of closure. From the top of this line you draw a line back to the starting point of this diagram, thereby creating a triangle with a series of verticals from its base. The intercept on each station's perpendicular marks the length of distance adjustment for that station; each such vertical line is that station's proportion of the total error. You mark, from the point of the trial plot, a distance along the line parallel to the error of closure equal to that found on the diagram described above. Having done this at each station (and this process applied to the final station brings its point in coincidence with the initial station) you replot the traverse in its adjusted form. This adjusted plot is the basis for further development of your map. (See Fig. 43.)

Fig. 42. Compass traverse: preliminary field sketch

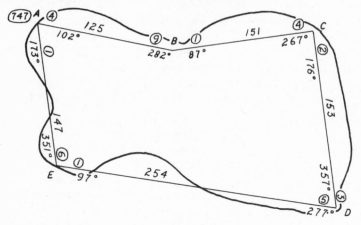

Fig. 43. Compass traverse: trial and adjusted plots

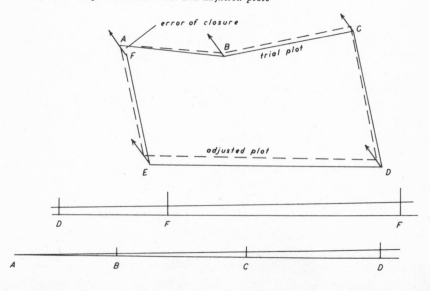

The foregoing method of adjusting the compass traverse plot is based on the assumption that errors will occur with equal frequency and equal degree in all legs. This is not likely to be true. Some legs will have been more difficult than others by reason of terrain or other problems and are to be suspected as having contributed more than their share of the error. You can take account of this possibility by proportional scaling of the line on the adjustment diagram. Make that segment of the line longer for the probably erroneous legs and shorter for those more likely to be true.

The error of closure for an open traverse is handled in virtually the same fashion. For the error to be known the traverse must proceed from a spot known from another survey to another spot known from another survey, assuming that other survey to have greater accuracy than your own. It may be advantageous to route your traverse in such a fashion as to touch such spots. They don't have to be confined to the termini of the survey; if you can tie in with known spots along the way, so much the better. The traverse plot is adjusted from known spot to known spot rather than from end to end in one piece. As with the closed traverse, a series of short lines parallel to the error of closure are ruled through the stations. A similar diagram is then constructed and the adjustment made as before.

It might appear that the adjustment of plot for distance and direction errors is going to introduce some problems with leveling. It will not, because you have simply determined the correct position of the places where levels were measured instead of altering these points.

The Sketching Traverse

It has been said that *Hamlet* without Hamlet leaves something to be desired. This is undoubtedly true of the play, but it is possible to run a compass traverse without a compass. Let us call the technique a sketching traverse for lack of a better name.

The sketching traverse is most likely to be done without any instrumentation whatsoever. So we will go all the way and assume that distances must be determined by pacing. This is surveying without instruments with a vengeance!

The surveyor uses only his notebook, a pencil, and a ruler. At each station the notebook is placed on the ground, the ruler placed upon it, and aligned with the last station. A line is then ruled. A foresight is then taken, aligning the ruler with the line of sight. (The ruler must lie across the end of the previous line.) Another line is ruled. Each line is marked to indicate which leg it is of the survey, and the distances from station to station are paced and noted. An effort is made to note the angles between successive legs of the survey and the lengths of these legs. Errors will tend to be self-cancelling and the whole result can be quite creditable. (See Fig. 44.)

The technique outlined above provides only the main traverse line. The surveyor will wish to note features as they occur along his route. These are best included by offset, which is figured by eye and paced off, or by the use of subsidiary triangles. In handling these triangles, the surveyor notes his pacing distance at an appropriate spot on the main survey line, marks the ground, and continues to a second such place which he marks too. He then paces the distance from each mark to the feature and notes these in his record. Subsidiary triangles are most appropriately used when the feature lies some distance off the traverse. A simple offset, in which the angle is not closely determined, can be in serious error if carried very far.

The sketching traverse is a technique which should be learned and practiced by every person who aspires to simple surveying skills. It may be practiced extemporaneously with materials normally at hand. The only preparation required is that of experience in pacing. Even this could be checked out after the fact because the distances are recorded in paces and sketch maps can be constructed on this basis. Only at a further level of refinement is there any need to convert the paced distances into an absolute measure, which can be done by simply adding a pace scale to the map.

The Plane Table Survey

Plane table surveying, as the name suggests, involves the use of a plane (or flat) table on which the alidade rests and on which the map is drawn. We have

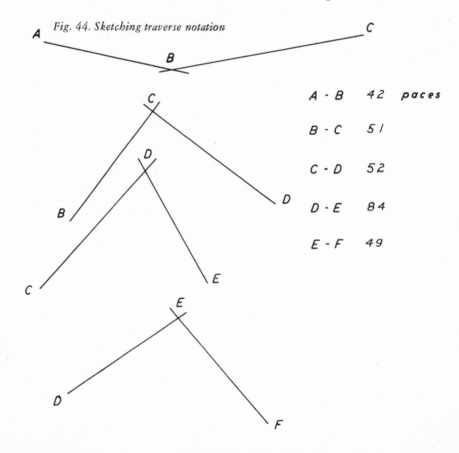

Fig. 44. Sketching traverse notation

A - B	42 paces
B - C	51
C - D	52
D - E	84
E - F	49

already discussed in detail most of the equipment appropriate to this style of surveying. Minimally, one needs the plane table drawing board and the alidade. Usually these are augmented by a tripod, a tape, and a leveling rod.

The equipment for plane table surveying is more bulky than most of that which we have already considered. This may present problems of transport. If there is any serious expectation of plane table surveying, it would be well to plan for it rather than to extemporize in the field. As has been explained, the drawing board can be a part of a planned packing box. The leveling rod scale can be a flexible rod. The alidade is compact, as is the tape. Only the tripod and the leveling head seem to be prima facie nuisances. If the tripod hardware were taken along and the surveyor were competent to make his own tripod or to direct a carpenter, then even this obstacle is small.

In general it may be said of the plane table survey that it gives the best result of any surveying style accessible to the amateur surveyor. For this reason it is recommended for consideration by all kinds of field workers who require complete, accurate surveys. If a sketch is all that is needed, then one of the styles mentioned above will probably suffice.

Some general preliminaries must be carried out before one is ready to start the survey. First, the tripod is set in place and the plane table drawing board is attached. The board is then set in a roughly level plane, using the tripod legs, their set in the ground, or the leveling head to achieve this orientation. The paper is then attached to the board. Professional surveyors' plane table drawing boards have screw studs recessed into the top, near the edges, to hold the paper. You will probably use draftsman's tape or masking tape to attach the paper. Thumbtacks or pins usually interfere with the alidade and are not recommended.

Because it is conventional to have the margins of a map oriented toward the cardinal compass points, you will turn the drawing board until one edge of the board (and presumably the paper) lies on a north-south line. Whether this is a long edge or a short edge of the rectangular board depends on the survey area. Professional boards may have a trough compass mounted in one of the long edges. As the north-south orientation is set, so also is the leveling of the board perfected. Once these are finished, you are ready to proceed with the survey.

The plane tabler's technique at the drawing board will ultimately be worked out as an individual style. However, it would not be amiss to offer some general suggestions.

As noted in the discussion of equipment, the plane table drawing board should be at such a height that the tabler can easily reach across it, yet so he does not have to stoop excessively when taking sights. For most people this would put the board at or slightly above waist height. You will not be able to lean on the board without disturbing its setting.

Sighting through an alidade, or its equivalent, can be quite tiring. Several factors to reduce fatigue are possible. Professional telescopic alidades have optional prism eyepieces so that you do not have to bring your eye to the level of the instrument, but may look down into it with a minimum of bending. You may wish to take a cue from this and similarly equip your homemade alidade. Knee bends to bring the eye level down to instrument level are tiring. It is suggested that the surveyor lean his torso laterally to lower the eye level. This maneuver has the merit of bringing the head over the board, and closer to the eyepiece of the instrument. It also keeps one shoulder and hand free above the level of the board to facilitate manipulation of the alidade. The right-handed person, using this lateral bend, will probably incline his torso to the left, keeping the right shoulder high.

For prolonged periods at the plane table the surveyor may desire a seat of some sort. Stools in the field are usually not the draftsman's type and many can prove to be quite unstable. A tall single-legged stool, or a shooting stick, is worth trying under these circumstances.

Handling of the alidade calls for some consideration. Normally the alidade is directed on the line of sight by pivoting it about the heel of its base plate. The rear end of the base plate is held approximately in place by using a finger or the butt of a pencil as the pivot point. The working edge of the alidade will, of course, be at the point on the map which represents the instrument station. Though marking this spot, and providing a pivot with a pin or brad is an attractive notion, it is not considered good practice. At the very least it will generate inaccuracies due to the measurable diameter of the pin. Your rays will originate from a circle, the circumference of the pin, rather than from a point as they should. Keep the proximal end (not the rear corner) of your working edge at the point and pivot about it.

The best practice is to always use one side of the alidade base (blade, shoe) for the drawing of rays. It is against this side that the accuracy of the instrument is tested. No matter how one may feel about the parallelism of the two edges of the blade, do not use both sides. A right-handed person will probably use the right side of the blade and most instruments are so planned.

Plane tabling is rather sensitive to weather conditions. First of all, humidity changes can make it difficult to keep the paper taut and even over the drawing board. Secondly, the plane table has to be protected from rainfall when in use. A large umbrella or even a tent fly may be rigged overhead, but it is a nuisance to tend to along with the details of surveying. Even when no rain is immediately in prospect, it would be wise to have a waterproof cover for the drawing board. It may save your developing map from disaster. Thirdly, plane tabling is a slow process in the field, although it does result in a semi-finished map, and requires the tabler to stand for long periods in one place. It does get rather cold in some places in winter, and very hot in summer.

There are three basic approaches to a plane table survey of an area: the radial method, the traverse method, and the triangulation method. Each has its proper uses and several may be combined in the pursuit of a given task. The surveyor should choose his method(s) to fit the job rather than the other way around.

In the radial method, the table is sited at a single place and not moved until the survey is completed. No other instrument station is ever used. The station may be either central to the area surveyed or to one side; even with the side location, it is still "radial." It must be, whatever the choice, so situated that all features of the area can be seen from the table. A flat site would be most suitable for a central location and this method. For an instrument station to one side, one might imagine that a site with an amphitheater-like arrangement would be easiest to handle, assuming that it does not have great differences in elevation.

Marked relief of the terrain, regardless of the plane table method employed, presents major difficulties with simple alidades. The leaf-sight alidades may not have slots long enough to enable sighting at substantial angles of elevation or depression. The best solution is to move the plane table and alidade to another location, closer to the level of the target.

Once the table is sited, a dot is marked on the paper to represent the location of the station. If the table is central, then the dot should be central. If the table is peripheral, then the dot should be near the proper border. From this dot, "rays" are drawn to the features which are to be surveyed. The ray is the line on the map drawn from station to feature. With the radial method it is necessary to indicate how far along this ray the feature is from the station. This entails measuring the distance and then scaling it along the ray on the map. The distance may be measured by any means at your command: pacing, use of a tape, use of stadia hairs (if any) in your alidade, or use of a range finder. If you are working alone, or even with one assistant, the radial method will involve a lot of footwork back and forth between instrument and targets. Any method of remote ranging of distance will reduce this walking. Therefore, the radial method is recommended primarily when these remote ranging techniques are available. (See Figs. 45 and 46.)

In addition to relating your surveying station to the features of your area by means of directions (rays) and distances, do not neglect to relate it to the larger world. Somewhere in your survey should be included information which will tie your survey to general landmarks. Sight from the table to at least one landmark which appears on general surveys of the region.

The traverse method of plane table surveying can be used for the surveying of a small, closed area, but is best adapted to extended cross-country surveys. You will observe that the plane table traverse method is surprisingly close to the sketching traverse method already described.

In the traverse method the table is moved from station to station, either along the route of a cross-country survey or around the boundary of a more restricted area. The traverse may either be closed (returning to its starting point) or open (not returning to any previous station). The procedure is about the same in both cases except for handling the error of closure. However, whether the traverse is open or closed, each successive station must be located in view of the last station. In other words, each station will be visible from two stations, the one just vacated and the one soon to be used.

To survey an area by the closed traverse method, the table is set up on your first station (perhaps a corner of the area) with one side of the drawing board roughly parallel to the adjacent boundary of the area. A dot to represent the first station is marked on the proper part of the paper. A sight is then taken on the second station. If no other target presents itself, the sight is taken to a rod (leveling or stadia) or a range (sighting-) pole held at the proper spot. Each station should be marked with a stake to facilitate precise location for the rodman or the surveyor. A ray is drawn from the first station in the direction of the second station. The distance is measured, by whatever means you choose to employ, and scaled off along this ray. The table is moved to the second station, now marked by a rod or range pole. To take this backsight the alidade is placed along the connecting ray and the drawing board turned until the sights of the alidade bear on the target. This alignment should be done with care so that the drawing board is oriented exactly as it was at the first station. A sight is taken to the third station, the ray marked, and so on. Each time the table is moved ahead and re-aligned. (See Fig. 47.)

The traverse method develops a line which is the main survey line. In itself, this method does little for details. Therefore, it is best to record the features en route by use of the radial method from one or more main survey stations. Depending on the relationship between the survey line and the areas of interest, the

Fig. 45. Radial plane tabling: central station

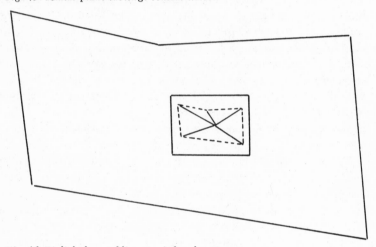

Fig. 46. Radial plane tabling: peripheral station

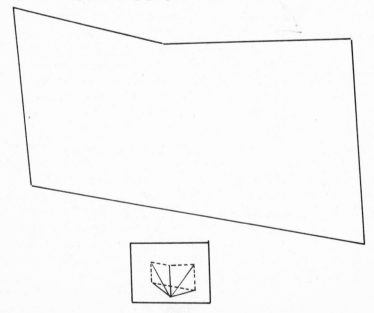

radial approach may be central or peripheral. It certainly can be both in a given survey. In cases in which the feature is visible from more than one main survey station, it may be to the surveyor's advantage to use the triangulation method which will be outlined in the next section.

The triangulation method of plane tabling is the third basic approach. While it can be used for the surveying of large areas, it is best suited for smaller ones in which every feature to be mapped is visible from most of the others. A flat site is ideal, as is a hillside of even slope. The triangulation method is really nothing more than a two-station traverse, with some definite advantages accruing from its use.

The two stations of this method are established at the ends of a straight line called a base line. While this arbitrary and imaginary line may theoretically be established anywhere, in practice it is often desirable to use as a base line some major feature of the area such as a boundary road or a fence. Select as your stations points which are in view of each other and from both of which the features to be

Fig. 47. Traverse plane tabling: closed traverse

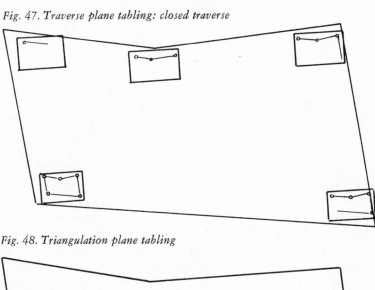

Fig. 48. Triangulation plane tabling

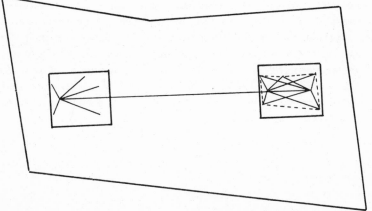

surveyed are visible. You will sight on each feature twice, once from each station. You will also sight from each station to the other. Plan accordingly in your choice of stations.

The table is set up at one station, at one end of your base line, oriented and leveled. Sights are taken successively with the alidade toward each feature to be mapped. Rays of indeterminate length are drawn toward each feature. No measurements of distance need be taken from the station to the features, and the rays accordingly are without scaled length for the moment. Each ray must be clearly identified so that it can be related to the second series of rays which will be drawn.

Once all the features to be mapped have been located directionally from the first station, the table is moved to the second station at the other end of the base line. It is critical that the distance between the two stations be carefully measured and scaled off. The table is set up and the drawing board is properly oriented by taking a backsight to the first station and then clamping it in place. A second series of rays are sighted and drawn from the point representing station two to the same features which were sighted from the first station. The intersection of two rays drawn to a given feature, one from each station, locates it on the map. No measuring, save that of the base line, is necessary with this method. (See Fig. 48.) Because so much of the surveying is done from the instrument, this method is a good one for the solitary surveyor or for a two-man surveying team.

Nothing has been said about leveling surveys combined with plane tabling. It certainly can be done, simultaneously if possible. With the radial method some kind of level sighting at a leveling rod can be used. The same rod may also mark the feature for the drawing of rays. If you are using an alidade with stadia hairs, and so engaging in distance ranging in this fashion, the target rod can do three things at once: mark the spot for direction; give you intercepts for distance ranging; and give you a level height for leveling. This type of operation is equal to that of professional surveying using professional equipment. It is doubtful that you will be handling these all at once.

With the traverse method of plane tabling, you may want to run your level sights from station to station to establish these levels. Backsighting is possible, in fact, recommended. Individual sights can be taken from each station to the features which are being mapped radially from there. The triangulation method offers a check on all of your levels if you want to take the time. The levels of the two stations should be carefully checked, at least as carefully as their distances. (Note that the fewer the number of measurements, the less chance there is for random averaging to even out mistakes.) From the first station you can take level sights to all features noted. The procedure is repeated from the second station. In the absence of other weightings of your data, you will probably use the average of the two measures as your record.

4

Many Hands

SURVEYING IN SEVERAL STYLES can be a one-man job, but generally the work is easier and quicker with an assistant. Among the obvious tasks for a surveyor's assistant (rodman) are the handling of one end of a tape, the holding of a leveling rod, and the pacing of distances. Of the several surveys we have considered, the sketching traverse, with paced distances, is best adapted for use by the lone surveyor. The compass traverse, again with pacing, would probably be next most easily accomplished alone. The full plane table survey, with levels, is hardly worth trying without assistance.

There are benefits to be gained from the use of assistants. First of all, the surveying goes faster in most cases. The amount of walking by the surveyor is much reduced. The results are likely to have greater accuracy when one person is not trying to be in two places at the same time. Second, once the assistant is trained he will serve as a check on the procedure followed by the surveyor. With two people watching the process, there is less chance for oversight or error. Third, the indigenous assistant will also be a local escort to the surveyor, validating his presence and explaining his activities to other people in the area. The measure of rapport and the entrée which may be gained with a local assistant is well worth the cost of his hire. It is possible that the work cannot be done otherwise. Finally, the assistant may be your source of native names for geographical features in the survey area.

The training of an assistant depends greatly on who this person may be. If your rodman will be another member of your field party, then he can certainly read through your instructional materials for himself. (It would be unfortunate if you had to put the rodman's job in the hands of someone who could make a greater research contribution. Consider this possibility as the last choice.) These materials could also be read by a native assistant who has had some secondary education. An exception to this possibility lies in the chance that his education has not included the language of these materials. In that case, do not spend your time translating the literature, but devote it instead to oral instruction.

The rodman should learn to hold a tape taut and on the mark. He should learn how to hold the tape with one hand and a plumb line with the other. He must know how to shift the tape so that fractions may be read at the front end. If he does not know how to read numbers, then some kind of improvisation will have to be made so that he can recognize, for example, the $3:4:5$ proportional points commonly used on the tape. A color-coded mark would seem an obvious choice, but beware of possible failure in the native culture to distinguish between certain colors, like the classic blue-green confusion. There may arise some problems in the leveling traverse when a rodman can not read numbers. Some system will have to be devised so that he can move forward of the instrument a distance equal to that from the last station to the instrument.

The rodman's task with a range pole is comparatively easy. He must hold it vertical and on the mark. Circumstances of terrain, distance, and vegetation may make the pole difficult to see. The rodman is then called upon to find an alternate location for the rod or to make it more visible by moving his hand or some other object in front of the pole.

The leveling rod presents about the same situation as does the range pole. It must be vertical and, as it is often in a wind, this is not as easy as it sounds. There are small levels which may be applied to the rod to assure verticality. The use of these is probably superfluous unless you have difficulty in getting your rodman to judge the matter for himself. The rodman must set the leveling rod where its base is properly located. He should understand the difference in procedure between precise levels, as at a bench mark, and general levels, such as those obtained for contours. The rod should, in the latter case, be rested on something representative of the general spot, not on a rock or log, nor in a hole.

Depending upon his ability to count, you may wish to train your rodman in pacing distances. It is his general function to do the "legwork" of a survey, and pacing is part of that aspect. Even though your mapping will likely be in feet or meters, the field notes ought to have the number of paces recorded. If both the surveyor and the rodman are doing the pacing some notational distinction will have to be made so that it can be told from the notes who paced what distance.

Though there may be a few abortive attempts to secure and train a rodman, once a satisfactory one has been found it would be well to keep him. Not only will he become more proficient at the tasks outlined above, but he can develop a discrimination between good and poor locations for sights. As soon as your trained rodman has this ability your job will be greatly reduced. Directions will be at a minimum.

Both the economic and psychological advantages which may be gained by the native rodman as a member of your surveying party are not to be overlooked. The training he receives is a very real part of his compensation and, if he loses his job through inefficiency, he has forfeited a great deal more than just his wages.

5

Surveying and Plotting Accuracy

THE DEGREE OF ACCURACY in a survey is a matter for serious consideration. In the first place, one can follow the puritanical adage that any job worth doing is worth doing well. Therefore, all surveying should be done with the maximum accuracy consistent with the methods available. It takes little longer to do a good job than a poor one. In the second place, one never knows that the uses to which one plans to put the survey will be the only ones for which it will eventually be employed. However, this zeal will inevitably be tempered by consideration of the limitations inherent in the processes of surveying and plotting.

In making his map, whether it is on the plane table drawing board in the field or produced from data brought home to the drafting table, the surveyor cannot plot a point nor end a line with greater accuracy than one-hundredth of an inch (0.01 in.). Even with a reasonably sharp pencil, the size of the dot or the width of a line will be at least that large under most circumstances. The accuracy limits of plotting set the limits on field accuracy. The two must be coordinate, for neither can improve the other.

For example, if the scale of the map were 1:1200, then 1 in. on the map would equal 1200 in. (100 ft) on the ground. One-hundredth of an inch on the map would equal 1 ft on the ground. If the surveyor were to make his field measurements to any unit smaller than the nearest foot, the effort would be superfluous. Similarly, if the scale were 1:120, the field measurements would be the nearest tenth of a foot.

This circumstance, it should be stressed, offers no excuse for careless surveying. It merely means that the surveyor should make no error on the ground which is greater than the maximum accuracy of his plotting on the map. Nothing would be gained by greater field accuracy.

A simple way of checking field accuracy would be to make a series of measurements of the distance between two features. If the maximum and minimum readings obtained do not vary from the average of these readings by more than half of the amount which would be scaled on the map as 0.01 in., one can rest assured that accuracy is adequate regardless of the method used.

Assume, for purposes of illustration, that your map is to be drawn at a scale of 1:600, that is 1 in. on the map equals 50 ft on the ground. For a given measurement you get a maximum of 164.7 ft and a minimum of 164.3 ft. The average is 164.5 ft and the difference from the average is 0.2 ft. One-hundredth of an inch on the map equals 0.5 ft on the ground; half of this is 0.25 ft. Therefore the accuracy of your measurements is adequate, as they differ by only 0.2 ft when 0.25 ft is permissible under the rule. What all this means is that you might be able to get more consistent measurements if you tried repeatedly, but you couldn't plot the measurement to reflect the great accuracy of field work.

Surveying stations are chosen with many desiderata in mind. You have to see certain other stations, previous or potential. You have to see more or less of the survey area. You want a location which does not pose problems for leveling. The station must be locatable with reference to bench marks of previous surveys. To this long list, one can add considerations of plotting accuracy as influencing the choice of stations.

The base line used in the triangulation and traverse methods of plane tabling must be of adequate length. (If you had not considered it before, the legs between successive traverse stations are actually base lines.) While there are no absolute standards to be applied, it is suggested that no base line be chosen which will not have a scalar length of 3 or more inches on the map.

If we again consider that 0.01 in. is the minimum plotting error to which we can aspire, we find that for the 3-in. base line this represents one three-hundredth (1/300) of the length of the line. For a base line represented by only a 1-in. line on the map, the 0.01-in. plotting figure would be one-hundredth of the line length, or three times as great an uncertainty as to the locations of the ends of the line.

Locations of stations are additionally influenced by their relationships to the features which are being mapped. In the plane table survey, as in some other types of surveys, the location of features is often determined by the intersection of two lines (or rays) on the map. This point will be most accurately located when the intersecting lines cross each other at right angles. The area of the intersection will then be as small, and as accurate, as is possible. If the lines, drawn at the minimum expectable width of 0.01 in., cross at 90°, the intersection will be a small square 0.01 in. on a side. As the angle of intersection is decreased from a right angle, the area of intersection increases; it changes in shape from a tiny square, as above, to a rhomboidal figure, and finally to a short line with tapered ends. (See Fig. 49.) It can be seen that the area of intersection could increase to the full length of the two lines if the angle between them were zero (0°).

Control of this angle of intersection is achieved through choice of the points from which the arcs are swung or the rays drawn. These points are the ends of this particular base line. To achieve the 90° angle of intersection the distance along the rays (or radii) should bear a certain ratio to the length of the base line, namely that of 14:20 (or more precisely, 14159:20000). This ideal cannot be achieved for each feature because it would require the establishment of a new base line. The three sketches in Figure 50 show the effect of varying the base line. The lengths of the rays are substantially the same in each case.

Practical considerations will make the ideal angle of intersection (at 90°)

of rays to all features difficult, if not impossible, of attainment. However, intersections at lesser angles are still reasonable. It is only when one finds a small included angle—perhaps less than 30°—that difficulties may arise.

Of course we are unable to choose, to any great degree, the features which we map. They are those of the landscape, of the settlement, or of the archeological site. However, there may be some choice possible in the selection of those features used as key points in the mapping process. Certainly the selection of base lines and the location of stations is entirely up to the surveyor. (Admittedly, there may be extraneous considerations. A prime station site might be the pediment for a shrine, and doubtless best avoided.) The skillful surveyor will exercise care in making this layout. It is for this reason, among others, that advance planning of the survey is stressed. A bit of time spent at the beginning may save hours of unnecessary work later on and improve the result immeasurably.

Among the strategies which may be employed, we might consider the

Fig. 49. Line intersections compared

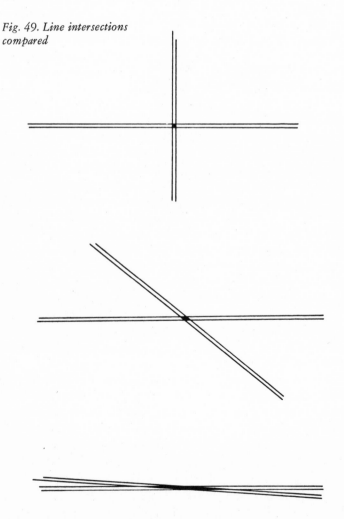

following as exemplary. While the base line for the two stations of the triangulation method of plane tabling may be set through the middle of the survey area, placing it to one side of the area and parallel to its long axis may present some advantages in keeping the ray intersection angles from becoming too small. If you try this out, you will find that there is a zone within the survey area, close to the base line, in which very low intersection angles will be the rule. Unless the survey area is quite large (which might favor use of the closed traverse method instead)

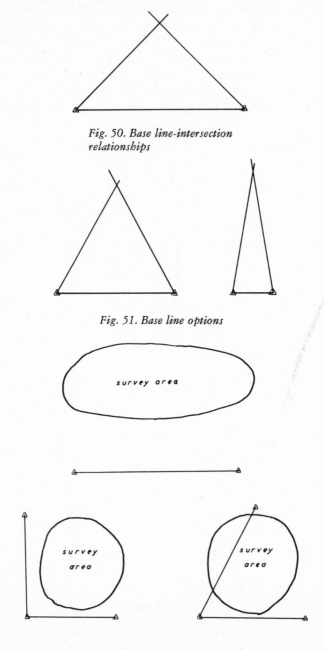

Fig. 50. Base line-intersection relationships

Fig. 51. Base line options

survey area

survey area

survey area

it is suggested that the base line be placed outside the area by a distance roughly equal to the width of the area proper. The length of the base line should, if possible, be equal to that of the area. (See Fig. 51.)

An alternative suggestion would be to use three instrument stations, with two base lines connecting them. The stations and their base lines would form either an "L"-shaped figure or an equilateral triangle. With the three-station setup, you could choose to take sights (and draw rays) from those two stations which give the most satisfactory intersection angles. (See Fig. 51.) This arrangement is also valuable in those cases in which all features of the area are not visible from both stations of the two-station system.

6

A Sample Survey

W E HAVE NOW DISCUSSED many of the techniques and requirements for amateur field surveying of sites. The application of these methods to any particular area—the basic method chosen, the scale, the appropriate accuracy, and the instruments used—will have to be determined by the surveyor. Not all of the techniques are suitable at the same time and to the same job. You have been given, along the way, a choice of techniques and some evaluation of their applications. The rest is up to you.

The choices should be governed by some overall considerations. Any good survey should show, for all important points and areas, the following: direction, distance, and level. Furthermore, the survey should be tied in to features appearing on larger, published maps or to those features which may be easily and unequivocally located by your successors.

To illustrate the application of a number of techniques to the mapping of a site, let us set up a hypothetical situation with which a surveyor might be faced. The area in question is a small archeological site located on the slope of a low ridge. (See Fig. 52.) There is a shallow ravine in the side of the ridge in which a clump of trees is growing. The spring around which they are clustered doubtless made the site attractive to its former occupants. However, the trees make it impossible to see all of the area from any single point; therefore, we will plan to use several instrument stations in the survey. If only one station were used, as is possible, it would be necessary to offset lines around the trees, complicating the survey.

We have decided to use a plane table survey because it can handle more specific points (features) in the survey area in less time than any of the other methods available to us. This decision fits in well with the need for two or more instrument stations; we can use an elaborated triangulation method or a limited traverse, whichever you prefer to call it.

The schematic plan of the survey area reveals that the use of any two stations—one and two or two and three—will leave some part of the area which cannot be seen from both stations. (The combintion of stations one and three is not possible because they are invisible with respect to each other.) Therefore, if we want to use triangulation to locate points in the survey area, we must add a third station. From these three stations many points can be located by three rays and there are none which cannot be located by two. The use of triangulation will eliminate the need for much measurement and help speed the survey along. (See Fig. 53.)

Our plane table drawing board gives us a working area, limiting the maximum size of the map to 15 by 25 in. This, considering the size of the area, means that we can use a scale of 1:240 (1 in. equals 20 ft). The plotting accuracy of such a scale would be 0.2 ft, assuming a dot and line limit of 0.01 in. This sug-

Fig. 52. Sample survey area

Fig. 53. Schematic plan of survey area

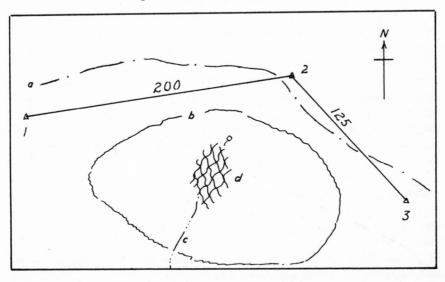

gests that measurements, when taken with the tape, be to the nearest tenth of a foot.

Station one is located close to the top of the ridge, beyond the western edge of the area. Station two is on top of the ridge, 200 ft east of station one; station three is near the ridge top and 125 ft southeast of station two. The merit of locating the stations generally above the area to be surveyed lies in the ease of leveling. The rod can project upward to the level of the instrument, but an instrument located toward the bottom of the slope might well be below the level of the foot of the rod.

The table is first set up at station one, oriented so that its long axis lies on an east-west line (parallel to the long axis of the survey area), and leveled. The position of the station is marked on what will be the northwest corner of the map.

Station one must then be tied in to major landmarks off the site. This can be done by a traverse—any one of several kinds—or may be done by sighting. We will assume that the landmarks are visible from the station and rays may be drawn toward them. This is done, and rays will later be drawn to the same marks from one or more of the other stations. The task of relating your survey to the larger world must not be overlooked in your eagerness to get to work on the area under consideration. It is better to do the tying-in process first rather than last. Even if the station which has been so related to the larger context proves ultimately to be unsuitable for your purposes, you will have tied-in a point in your survey area. If the station is relocated, you will include this tied-in point in the new survey scheme. Nothing has been lost and no motion wasted.

The position of station two should be determined and a sight taken toward it. The distance between the two stations is carefully measured and scaled off along the ray from station one to station two. Station three will be located later when the table has been moved to station two. For the present it is invisible behind the clump of trees. At this time the surveyor will have to decide whether he is going to map levels using contours or spot elevations. The site has not been excavated so no significant cultural features have yet been revealed. Further, its surface is pretty uniform, lacking sharp natural features which might be chosen for spot elevations. Therefore, the surveyor decides to survey for contour lines. If the elevations of individual features are wanted later these can be determined from the contours, while the reverse is not possible.

The surveyor, or his rodman, picks out a series of somewhat arbitrary points over the area to be mapped. In themselves there is nothing outstanding about these spots but they can be chosen so as to facilitate the determination of contours, for example, the leading edge of a slight ridge down a slope, the inward fold of a gully or ravine, and so on. If these points can be kept on approximately the same level or elevation, as determined by eye, they will be easier to use when drawing the contour lines. Because our site is small and the slope gentle we will use a 2-ft contour interval. The choice of contour interval is related to the character of the area, the degree of detail desired on the resulting map, the use to which the survey will be put, and the diligence of the surveying crew. The surveyor will have to use his own judgment and make his own compromises.

The rodman then moves over the area to be covered, placing his leveling rod at each of the chosen points in turn. The instrument man (surveyor) sights at the rod with his alidade and draws a ray from the station toward the rod. Each survey point where the rod is placed should be marked with a stake so that it can be relocated when the instrument has been moved to station two or station three. In addition to noting the direction of each sight, the surveyor will read the level on the rod. It is assumed here that his alidade indicates level as well as direction. If this is not the case, then he may augment the plane table and alidade with a hand level of some kind. It is probably adequate to take mostly foresights with the level (unless levels are an exceedingly important part of the survey), with only occasional backsights taken on checkpoints throughout the area. The height of the alidade or hand level above the ground at station one must be found by direct measurement and entered into the record.

As a time- and step-saving measure, the surveyor may wish to locate several points along each ray. The bearing will, of course, be the same for all, but the levels will not. The rodman can work his way along a line away from the instrument, move laterally to another bearing, and come back along the new line. By this time your developing survey map will look like Fig. 54. You have located a series of points in terms of their direction and elevation relative to station one, but not for distance which will be gotten through triangulation from station two or station three. Each ray is numbered to correspond with the number of the point-marking stakes and will have along it the measured elevation of the points along that ray.

Satisfied that you have completed all the necessary steps at station one, you uproot your plane table and move it to station two. Here the drawing board is leveled and then oriented so that the alidade, resting along the ray connecting the positions of station one and station two, is aimed exactly at the rod, or ranging pole, held at the stake marking the site of station one. This process of re-orienting the board must be done with great care or else your entire map will be in error. This is the same orienting technique which is used in the plane table traverse and triangulation surveying methods. Even though you used the compass to orient the board initially, at station one, use a backsight from station two, because it will give more accurate results and compensate for possible instrument errors.

The surveying process is continued from station two by taking a second set of sights at those points already located from station one. The rays drawn from station two may be very short ones, just long enough to mark the intersections with rays previously drawn through these points. Unless you are very unsure of your technique, it is not necessary to repeat the leveling sights for these points.

In addition to the cross-sights taken on points sighted from station one, you now take a second series of sights on points lying to the east of the trees. These are invisible from station one; so this is the first set of rays drawn to these points. The rodman will operate much as before and mark each point properly. The elevations of these new points must be found. Remember that these elevations must be referred to the same base level, or datum plane, as those taken from station one. The use of a constant correction factor, based on the difference in elevation between the two stations, will probably be the easiest way to manage this situation. Now

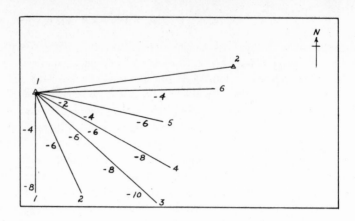

Fig. 54. First rays from Station 1

Fig. 55. The second set of rays

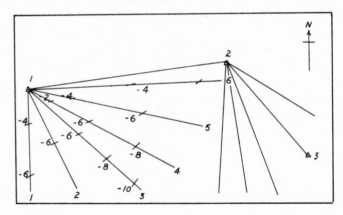

Fig. 56. Contours sketched

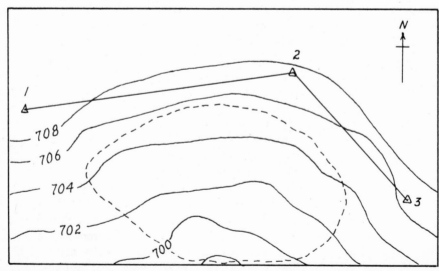

the map will look something like Fig. 55, from which many details have been omitted for the sake of clarity.

Before the plane table is moved to the third station, the cross-sights on landmarks which tie in the survey should be taken. The third station is located. The ray is drawn and the measured distance between stations is scaled off on the map. The plane table is then moved to station three, leveled, and oriented by back-sighting to station two. A series of cross-sights is taken on the points surveyed from station two. Perhaps some cross-sights will be taken on points directionally located from station one which were not also visible from station two.

We now have a series of definitely located points and their elevations. The datum for the elevations is the level of station one. The next step is to draw in the contours. These are sketched, in the field, by connecting all points of equal elevation, with constant reference being made to the appearance of the terrain in order to take note of minor differences not shown by the measured levels. The sketching of contours is somewhat difficult for the inexperienced, but the task is eased by having many points of recorded elevation for reference. It is better to take too many elevation and direction sights than to take too few, if you want an accurate map. The sketching process may well include the limits of the site and the clump of trees in this case. (See Fig. 56.)

You have now made a map of the survey area using some of the techniques which have been discussed. There are, as you should now be aware, still other techniques which might have been employed. It is improbable that any surveying project, however complex or fanciful, would employ every conceivable method.

7

Graphic Display of Data

THE TRADITIONAL FORM for the display and summarization of survey data is a map. The complexity of a map may be a measure of its completeness, but not necessarily of its utility. For example, a detailed French road map shows not only the road net, character of the road, distances, towns, and political boundaries, but more than thirty other kinds of information. If studied carefully this map is tremendously informative. At the same time, it is impossible for a driver to use while the automobile is in motion. The moral of this tale is that the map must be suited to its use. While there are some considerations which are specific for each case, there are others more generally valid, and an effort will be made to confine the following remarks to the latter sort.

Though the comments here will be directed toward aspects of map drafting, it should not be forgotten that some surveying data is appropriately shown by graphs or charts. A profile of levels, developed from the recording scheme for a leveling traverse may be substantially more useful than a map of contours or spot elevations. The profile's emphasis can be enhanced by using different vertical and horizontal scales, as is usually the case.

The scale of your field map may be dictated by the size of your plane table drawing board measured against the size of the survey area. You usually have to get the entire survey on one sheet of paper, and this is one of the few limitations of the plane table method. With a bit of planning it may be possible to continue the survey onto a second or third sheet of paper by using the traverse technique and picking up the ray of the base line as a backsight on the new sheet of paper. When the map is ultimately drawn on the drafting table, it will be put together, literally or figuratively, using this direction and distance between the linking stations.

The scale of the finished map, done on the drafting table, is not usually limited by mechanical considerations; we can make it as large or as small as desired. There are some scales which are customary. It seems unlikely that an amateur surveyor will cover an area more than a few miles long in any direction, with the consequence that the scale of 1:62500 (approximately an inch to the mile) will be the smallest conceivably employed. In fact, the scale of some U.S. Geological Survey topographic maps, at 1:24000 (or about 2⅝ in. to the mile), might still be too small for practical use. The use of a scale related to this figure has much to recommend it. However, the choice of scale cannot be arbitrary, nor necessarily conformist.

The map's scale is also related to the amount of detail which it is expected to show. If the map of a town is to show, to scale, the width of streets, then this must be taken into account. Suppose that the town is a mile square and you wish to map it on a paper 18 in. square. The minimum street width is 20 ft. Can this be shown and at what scale? In the first place, the size of the town (1 mile) and of paper (18 in.) set a preliminary scale of 1:3600 (1 in. to 300 ft, rounded off from 1:3520). The maximum practical accuracy of plotting is to 0.01 in.; at the projected scale of 1:3600, this equals 3 ft. The 20-ft street would scale to be about 0.07 in. wide. Therefore the proposed scale is feasible. Following the calculations in the section on accuracy, the permissible error for field measurements at this scale is ½ of 3 ft or 1.5 ft. Measurements taken to fractions of a foot cannot be plotted although they may, at some points in the survey, be noted in another fashion.

In this, the Age of the Copying Machine, it would be well to consider how you are going to note your map scale. For all that we have been talking about scales of an inch to the mile, or similar proportions, it had better not be noted in this form on the map. Because, if the map is reproduced by any optical method, its true size is likely to be changed. And this, of course, will destroy the correctness of any verbal statement such as "one inch equals two hundred feet." Consequently, use only the fractional notation, such as 1:2400, or the graphic representation of scale by a bar showing the scalar length of a distance. Either of these representations will pass through enlargement or reduction without harm.

In regard to reductions, it might be well to note that maps are usually reduced when they are printed. This smoothes the roughness of lines and lettering. It makes drafting easier at a larger size. However, it can make some of the fine details disappear and it can make some smaller items virtually microscopic in reproduction. Therefore, plan ahead. An aid to planning and visualizing the end result is a reducing glass, an item like a magnifying glass in reverse. Viewing your work through the reducing glass gives a more realistic result than squinting at it from a distance. The investment is small and the returns great if you are going to do much drawing for publication. This piece of equipment is, of course, for the drafting room, not for the field.

The initial drafting room layout of a compass traverse is easiest done on graph paper. This means that the protractor does not have to be constantly controlled by a T-square. Angles can easily be read off the grid of the paper. The grid may also be used, in some directions, as a means of scaling distances. One probably does not want the finished map to appear on graph paper. The simplest and most accurate transfer from graph paper to plain paper is by pricking through the major points with a needle.

Field notations will be made in pencil, with one fine-pointed pencil to draw lines and a shorter-pointed one for notes. Even though pencils will smudge with rubbing and have other drawbacks, there is nothing which will beat them in the long run. The pencil lines which were used to conduct a plane table survey will ultimately be erased; you do not want the map all cluttered with rays. A pocket knife will sharpen the wood of your pencil and a bit of sandpaper glued to a tripod leg can help give it a fine point.

Ink is appropriate to the finishing of maps on the drafting table. This should be India ink, not to sustain tradition, but because this carbon-base ink will reproduce best. Ballpoint pens are not acceptable. They use various dyes, rather than a true ink, to make their mark, and will not reproduce by some processes. Additionally, ballpoint pens shed blobs of ink along their lines and at the ends of lines. If you want something which approaches the convenience of the pocket pen, then use special India ink of the fountain pen type in your fountain pen. You may prefer to use one of the pens with a hollow, tubular point. These last are not very good for ruling lines, but they will make a uniform line regardless of the direction of motion.

Another reason for finishing a map with ink is that it offers ready control of line width, hence of emphasis. You do not want each line on your map to be the same as all the rest. A pencil does not give very good line width control, but the ruling pen is made for the task. Similarly, if other pens are used the proper nib can be chosen.

Lettering on maps often proves a headache for amateur draftsmen. For years there have been various lettering guides available. They come in two basic styles. The first uses a template on which there rides a stylus. The stylus is linked, by being mounted on the same body, to a pen point which makes the actual mark. The points are changeable to control the line width and the relation between stylus and pen can be altered (in some models) to change the slope of the letters. The second style is basically a stencil through which the fine pen point passes. The stencil is so constructed that it does not bear directly on the paper at the point of lettering so that there is no danger of smudging the results. The points of the stencil pens are changeable, but more limited in scope due to the necessity of fitting through the stencil's slots. Separate stencils are needed for vertical and slant letters.

Lately there have appeared on the market several forms of transfer letters which, when carefully applied, can produce very professional results. The letter is printed, in a special ink, on the underside of a transparent film. It is held on the paper, properly located, and the upper side of the film is rubbed at that point. The letter transfers, or reflexes, onto the surface of the paper. Lettering of various styles and sizes is available in this new medium.

Typewriters with interchangeable type or special fonts may be the basis for map lettering, especially for wordy portions such as legends. The material, typed out on a separate sheet, is cut into bits and attached at the proper places. Dry mounting tissue or rubber cement is probably the best adhesive medium. However, this approach should be used only when the map is going to be reproduced by photographic or similar means rather soon after its drafting. Otherwise, these bits and pieces may come off through handling or aging and spoil the map.

Finally, something might be said about preserving your map. This is particularly important if the product is to be used repeatedly in the field as, for example, the notation medium for an extended survey.

The map can be mounted on cloth, if you wish. The process which follows is quite wet and you should use it only if the map's marks will not bleed or run. Printed maps work well. The cloth base is either unbleached muslin or linen (depending on your affluence) which is stretched taut over a table or drawing board. It would be wise to wax the table surface or otherwise provide a parting agent so that the mounted map is not mounted on the table. A wheat paste is prepared; wallpaper paste is very acceptable. The paste is spread in a substantial coat on the cloth. The paper is thoroughly wet, on both sides, by a quick immersion in water and placed on the pasted cloth. The excess paste is then rolled out from under the paper. The paper may stretch during the rolling, so have an adequately large area prepared. The whole assemblage is then allowed to dry completely before being removed from the table or board. The resulting map is stiff, but not unmanageable.

You may want to try mounting, in advance, the paper on which your map will be drawn. Possibly this will give greater dimensional stability to the paper when it is placed on the plane table drawing board. It is certainly worth a try if you have problems with humidity changes.

Some of the handling problems arising from the stiffness of the mounted map can be overcome by the dissected mode of mounting. The procedure is as before except that the map has been previously cut into even-sized pieces. When the wet pieces are smoothed onto the pasted cloth a space, about 0.2 in., is left between adjacent pieces. The mounted map can be folded repeated at these joints without harming the paper in the least. You will gauge the size and number of your pieces according to the folded size you desire. Such a map is best folded in accordion fashion rather than over and over along a straight line. This prevents bulking at the folds. An even number of segments will make it possible to fold the working side of the map inside and have it protected in the closed position.

Another preservative treatment for a map is to coat it with boiled linseed oil. The map is tacked out flat and oiled. It is then allowed to dry for several days, during which time the oil oxidizes and hardens somewhat. The treated map is resistant to water and soiling, but will take pencil marks. This process is most suitable for a finished map and may be applied to maps on which the colors might run if wet with water. Presumably other oils might be used in the absence of boiled linseed oil. Under some field circumstances you may have difficulty securing the oil. Something quite usable might be decanted or pipetted off the upper layers of an unstirred can of oil-base paint. About 75 percent of the liquid in the paint is linseed oil.

All of the materials mentioned so far—cloth, paste, and oil—are likely to be found in the field. If you wish to make advance preparation for map protection, you can take along any of the common artist's and draftsman's fixatives. The fixative liquid and an atomizer are lighter and have greater coverage than the same gross weight of supplies in an aerosol can.

8

Conclusion

PRESUMABLY, if you have been able to follow the discourse to this point, you are equipped with a knowledge of elementary surveying. However, in the same way that it is doubtful that you would readily learn to swim or to ride a bicycle solely from written sources, so it is improbable that you can file away your knowledge until confronted by a survey in the field. It would be very wise to try several techniques and accumulate some experience in advance of the real thing.

Practice, under conditions which approximate those anticipated in the field, will develop a sureness of hand and a familiarity which reduces error through oversight. The practice of surveying is like that of photography. You can do both "by the numbers," but to do so requires concentration which should be focused on other aspects of your research. The running of your survey, like the operation of a camera, ought to become second nature.

Experience in surveying will develop a discrimination between alternative techniques. It is inconceivable that you will like all approaches equally. With some you will feel more at ease, more confident of results. Experience will help you to arrive at these judgments. Similarly, experience and the choices between techniques will clarify your equipment list. You may, for example, become convinced that your eyesight makes mandatory the use of optical sighting instruments. You may decide that a full-fledged survey of your research area will take more time than you have to devote to it. Consequently, you modify the research plan and timetable. You realize that you will have to hire a field assistant if you are going to survey; his wages must be in your budget. You plan to ship more field equipment in advance of your own departure. You cut down on and reorganize your baggage to include surveying equipment. Or you find, to your pleased surprise, that everything needed for the style of survey planned will be available from local sources in the field.

Though some of the survey methods detailed above are self-checking, it is best to gain experience in known territory. You should find an area which has been previously surveyed in a style corresponding to the one which you wish to learn. The choice of your practice survey area will be conditioned, in part, by the size of your actual field area. If the field survey will cover miles of land, then your practice survey should do so too. A previous survey of many large practice areas is easily acquired in the United States. Secure a U.S. Geological Survey map of the region at a scale of 1:62500 (the 15-minute series) or 1:24000 (the 7.5-minute series). On these you can find check points for your traverses, confirmation of your elevations, and other needed details. These maps are usually sold by blueprint companies and in college bookstores. Information about them is always available from the State Geologist in your state capital.

If you propose to survey a smaller area at a larger scale, a confirming survey may be found for a recent subdivision. In most of these the developer must file, with governmental authorities (such as a zoning commission), a thorough survey of the proposed plan. If the proposal and the outcome are the same, you will find in this a good comparative source. A professional surveyor, if you can convince him of your intentions, may be willing to furnish, at the cost of a copy, a set of plans for an area of this kind. This would be particularly true of a subdivision which is filled and considered finished business by the surveyor and developer.

Surveying of various kinds is taught at many colleges and universities, commonly in engineering schools or in departments of geology and geography. The students in these courses have surveyed, time and again, some portion of the campus or other test area. Probably you can gain the use of the master survey to check your own results.

If all of these sources of confirming data fail you, then try to survey the same area using several different techniques. The results of these may then be compared. Whatever the approach, do not neglect to spend some time familiarizing yourself with field surveying and map drawing. You would not, one assumes, undertake linguistic or musical field recording without prior experience under more controlled conditions. There is no excuse for lack of preparedness in surveying.

Advice on the choice of survey methods is of little value in the abstract. The surveyor should be sufficiently familiar with several techniques so as to form a sound opinion on their applicability in a given situation. In general it may be suggested that the chain survey is best suited to simple, though careful, surveying of a smaller area. The compass traverse and the sketching traverse are suited to careful and summary surveys, respectively, of a cross-country nature. The plane table survey is best suited to an intensive survey of a limited area. The choice may be dictated as much by available equipment as by any other consideration. Each method undertaken with care, can produce creditable results.

Throughout, a stress has been placed on field accuracy with a caution about the limits imposed by plotting accuracy. This sentiment does not preclude the use of sketching to note details. The task would be endless if each and every detail were to be "shot in" with the care taken for major features. Sketching does not take much time and enables the surveyor to include secondary details. One or two corners of a simple building will locate it adequately for most purposes. The same would be true of a street intersection if the street widths are generally known.

Surveying is, somewhat surprisingly, not known as a hobby in the United States, although Britain does boast some amateur surveyors. This is hardly the place to argue the recreational merits of surveying, but it can be a source of pleasure to see a closure made with small error or to have one's own map of a park. As with some other recreations, surveying offers an opportunity for outdoor activity with an element of self-testing and intellectuality thrown in for good measure.

Comment has been made before about the contributions which a survey, and the resulting map and other knowledge, may add to a field study. For those who are visually-minded, the assistance to comprehension is great. For those who seek thoroughness of research, the care of a job well done is reflected in a survey. Although an accepted part of the research of the archeologist, surveying can enrich the work of all branches of anthropology.

Recommended Reading

Debenham, Frank, 1955, *Map Making,* 3d ed. Glasgow: Blackie and Son.
An excellent source on simple surveying, primarily avocational, by a professional geographer. References are strongly British.

Detweiler, A. Henry, 1948, *Manual of Archaeological Surveying.* New Haven, Conn.: American Schools of Oriental Research.
The only manual devoted exclusively to archeological surveying. Quite technical, very thorough. Contains notes on sketching archeological remains. For use on large Near Eastern sites, but adaptable elsewhere.

Heizer, Robert F., and John A. Graham, 1967, *A Guide to Field Methods in Archaeology,* rev. ed. Palo Alto, Calif.: National Press.
Contains a section on archeological surveying similar to those found in many field methods guides.

Pannell, J. P. M., 1966, *The Techniques of Industrial Archaeology.* Newton Abbot, Eng.: David and Charles.
Has a short chapter on surveying, but a great deal of the book is useful in making descriptive studies.

Equipment Sources

The following firms, listed alphabetically, are mentioned for the convenience of the reader and their inclusion does not imply endorsement of their products. In many cases their products may be secured through college bookstores and blueprint or engineering companies. Unless otherwise noted the companies offer a general line of surveyor's and draftsman's equipment and supplies.

William Ainsworth and Sons, Inc., 2149 Lawrence Street, Denver, Colorado 80205 (makers of the Brunton pocket transit).

Charles Bruning Co., 1800 West Central Road, Mount Prospect, Illinois 60056 (about 100 branch offices).

Eugene Dietzgen Co., 2425 North Sheffield Avenue, Chicago, Illinois 60614 (22 branch offices).

Edmund Scientific Co., 103 East Gloucester Pike, Barrington, New Jersey 08007 (gadgets, prisms, levels).

W. and L. E. Gurley, Station Plaza, Troy, New York 12180 (transits, alidades, magnetic compasses).

Keuffel and Esser Co., 303 Adams Street, Hoboken, New Jersey 07030 (19 branch offices).

A. Lietz Co., 840 Post Street, San Francisco, California 94108 (drafting supplies).

Frederick Post Co., 700 Northwest Highway, Des Plaines, Illinois 60016.

Silva, Inc., 700 Ridgeway Boulevard, La Porte, Indiana 46350 (magnetic compasses).

Stanley Tools, 666 Myrtle Street, New Britain, Connecticut 06053 (carpenters' levels, squares).

Index

83

STUDIES IN ANTHROPOLOGICAL METHOD

GENERAL EDITORS

George and Louise Spindler

Stanford University

WINSTON, INC.

York 10017

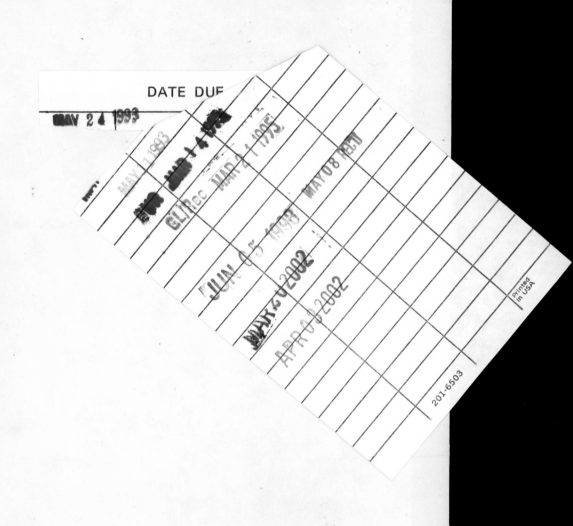